HERAKLES

PASSAGE
OF
THE
HERO
THROUGH
1000
YEARS
OF
CLASSICAL
ART

ESSAYS

KARL GALINSKY
KEVIN LEE
WILLIAM MULLEN
BERNARD STAMBLER
JAIMEE PUGLIESE UHLENBROCK

ENTRIES

DAVID GORDON MITTEN
ALAN SHAPIRO
JAIMEE PUGLIESE UHLENBROCK
CORNELIUS VERMEULE

JAIMEE PUGLIESE UHLENBROCK

HERAKLES
PASSAGE
OF
THE
HERO
THROUGH
1000
YEARS
OF
CLASSICAL
ART

Aristide D. Caratzas, Publisher New Rochelle, New York
The Edith C. Blum Art Institute, Bard College Annandale-on-Hudson, New York

1986

Herakles: Passage of the Hero through 1000 Years of Classical Art was produced in coordination with the exhibition of the same name at the Edith C. Blum Art Institute, Bard College, March-May, 1986.

Aristide D. Caratzas, Publisher
Caratzas Publishing Co., Inc.
481 Main St., P.O. Box 210
New Rochelle, N.Y. 10802

ISBN: 0-89241-420-0 (Cloth)
      0-941276-07-4 (Paper)
Library of Congress Catalog Card Number: 85-080655

Book design by Maj-Britt Hagsted
Color separations and printing by Studley Press, Dalton, MA

Printed in the United States of America

CONTENTS

FOREWORD

If mythology is a metaphor expressive of the hope, faith, and mystery of human destiny, then the characters who populate mythology's dramatic narrative can be viewed as manifestations of these psychological functions. The hero myth is particularly revealing of the urgings and stirrings of the human psyche. Not only did versions of this myth appear millennia ago in many diverse cultures from Mesopotamia to Polynesia, but these tales continue to prevail to this day. Although the details vary, the essential characteristics remain consistent. The hero is identified with a great quest. He is often aided by some supernatural force so that although he must penetrate into a hostile zone, the success of his journey is preordained. Once he has entered the dreaded territory, he accomplishes some extraordinary feat. Upon his return, news of his astonishing victory is shared with the community. In this way, the hero has both strengthened and renewed society. His survival is evidence of the fact that there is no cause for fear; beyond terror lies either triumph or rebirth.

The psychological requirement that the hero legend addressed is but one aspect of its universal and popular appeal. It also offers an action-packed adventure story that is sure to capture the human imagination. There is an irresistible allure in the extraordinary creatures and challenges the hero encounters. Such stories release the audience from the tedium of daily existence and propels it into a rite of battle, feasting, excess, and improbability. The hero performs, in the words of Joseph Campbell, "a pageant of marvels." He enters the arena with swords and a swagger and thoughts of conquest, and these thoughts are rarely unfulfilled. The exaltation of the hero is calculated in terms of power, profit and action. His glory is a metaphor for the transcendence of danger and the exhilaration of achievement. Most commonly, these qualities are related to the male character. These myths set a standard for male excellence: courage, pride, and strength.

By all of these standards, Herakles is not only the original, but also the quintessential hero. He emerged in ancient times and seems destined to survive, if only by association, as long as there are trials to endure and images of valor to conjure.

But even as Herakles/Hercules as hero-image has survived, the essential elements of his character have undergone a remarkable transformation over the course of history. His rich biography has provided each successive generation with the opportunity to select elements most relevant to its specific circumstances. Herakles has defined the meaning of labor, challenge, and duty. He reveals the relationship between the virtue of excellence and the virtue of moderation, between pride and modesty, honor and guilt, free will and destiny. At the same time, Herakles exemplifies the role of man in society, within the family, and as interactor with the gods.

All of these issues are reflected in the current exhibition. The works of art depict the reinterpretation of this myth over the course of twelve hundred years — from 600 B.C. to 600 A.D. These beautiful objects tell and retell the Herakles legend which unfolds in a continual and fascinating metamorphosis. They show Herakles' godly virtues and his mortal fallibilities. His passage is not only a journey from adventure to adventure across the ancient world, but also through centuries of time as the details are replayed.

While the hero in today's culture has lost direct reference to gods and goddesses, his role seems hardly to have been rationalized. It remains, to this day, the romanticized embodiment of the lone warrior whose destiny is to embody the struggle against some alien element in society. The hero in American history has overcome the dangers of the great frontier whether in the exploration of the West or of outerspace. He has been the captain of industry, the athlete who has surpassed all performance records, or the soldier who demonstrates uncommon valor. In all cases, such heros represent the epitome of manly perfection, attaining the glory that makes them worthy of the term 'hero.'

This exhibition celebrates noble qualities and testifies to the accomplishments of classical Greece, which have set an example of artistic excellence for more than two thousand years.

Linda Weintraub, Institute Director, The Edith C. Blum Art Institute

ACKNOWLEDGMENTS

To the extermination of the Nemean Lion, the seering of the Lernaean Hydra, the capture of the wild boar of Erymanthus, and the gathering of the golden apples of the Hesperides, etc., can now be added a thirteenth labor of Herakles. It consists of assembling over 60 choice representations of this mythological hero in classical art from thirty prestigious collections across the United States. The task has, indeed, been Herculean, and could not have been achieved, in the absence of Herakles himself, without the cooperation and participation of a whole team of experts. The resulting exhibition and its accompanying text make evident the scholarship, talent, and skill of each member of this team. The Edith C. Blum Art Institute is privileged to have worked with such a distinguished group of individuals.

On behalf of the many visitors with whom we will share this special exhibition, I would like to express sincere gratitude to Jaimee Uhlenbrock, Associate Professor of Classical Art and Archaeology, State University of New York at New Paltz. She has been commited to the project from its inception to its culmination, and has shown exceptional patience and vigilance in guiding the project over a long, but rewarding journey. I am also grateful to David Gordon Mitten, The James Loeb Professor of Classical Art and Archaeology, Harvard University; Cornelius Vermeule, Curator, Department of Greek and Roman Antiquities, Museum of Fine Arts, Boston; Alan Shapiro, the Department of Humanities, Stevens Institute of Technology; Karl Galinsky, Chairman and James R. Dougherty, Jr. Centennial Professor, Department of Classics, The University of Texas at Austin; Bernard Stambler, Professor Emeritus, Manhattan Community College; Kevin Lee, Center for Hellenic Studies, Harvard University; and William Mullen, Associate Professor of Classics, Bard College. They generously shared the knowledge they have accumulated throughout the course of their professional lives.

Thanks are due as well to Evelyn Harrison, The Edith Kitzmiller Professor of the History of Fine Arts, New York University; James McCredie, Director New York University; Andrew Clark, Education Assistant and Staff Lecturer, Department of Public Education, The Metropolitan Museum of Art; Thomas Solley, Curator, Indiana University Art Museum; Susan Matheson, Yale University Art Gallery; Robert Guy, Art Museum, Princeton University; Valerie Hutchinson, Iconographicum Lexicon, Rutgers University; Donald Ringe, Associate Professor of Classics, Bard College (1984-1985). They all provided much appreciated guidance and went well beyond the call of duty in suggesting additions to the exhibition and in planning the presentation of the works of art.

I would also like to thank Bard College President Leon Botstein, Executive Vice President Dimitri Papadimitriou, and Board of Overseers Chairman Wilbur Friedman, who guided the project through its many phases, and Iris Kufert, Mirko Gabler, Ann Gabler, Judy Samoff, Tina Iraca Green, Donald Bennett, Ed Martin, and Lucy Ferris, who contributed the panoply of skills required to produce this exhibition and the accompanying catalog.

This exhibition was supported, in part, by public funds from the New York State Council on the Arts and by private funds from the Samuel H. Kress Foundation.

LIST OF LENDERS

The American Numismatic Society, New York City
Art Museum, Princeton University, Princeton
Bowdoin College Art Museum, Brunswick, Maine
Brooklyn Museum, Brooklyn
Cleveland Museum of Art, Cleveland
James Coats Collection, New Haven
Torkom Demirjian, Ariadne Galleries, New York City
M. H. De Young Memorial Museum, San Francisco
Jerome Eisenberg, New York City
J. Paul Getty Museum, Malibu
Museum of Art, Santa Barbara
Indiana University Art Museum, Bloomington
Lowie Museum of Anthropology, University of California, Berkeley
Department of Classics, Harvard University, Cambridge
Archer M. Huntington Art Gallery, University of Texas, Austin
Yale University Art Gallery, New Haven
San Antonio Museums Association, San Antonio
Wadsworth Athenaeum, Hartford
Metropolitan Museum of Art, New York City
Rhode Island School of Design Art Museum, Providence
Worcester Art Museum, Massachusetts
The University Museum, University of Pennsylania, Philadelphia
Mount Holyoke College Art Museum, Holyoke
Virginia Museum of Fine Arts, Richmond
Museum of Art and Archaeology, University of Missouri, Columbia
Museum of Fine Arts, Boston
Robert Miller, New York City
Dorothy Pack, Scarsdale
Alan Safani, New York City
Vassar College Art Gallery, Poughkeepsie

Statuette of Herakles with the skin of the Nemean Lion. Early
Roman Imperial, first century A.D. Bronze. H. 16.4 cm.
Collection of Robert Haber.

HERAKLES: LABORS, WORKS, DEEDS

Herakles the Theban—or, according to some, the Tyrinthian—was the son of Zeus and the mortal woman Alkmene. Conceived amidst cosmic miracles when three nights became one and the moon rose twice, he was destined by his father to be the greatest hero the world had ever known. The goddess Hera, wife of Zeus, learned of her husband's infidelity with Alkmene and, with a relentless hatred, set out to plague Herakles from birth with mortal danger, madness, and tragedy. Ironically, the fame won by Herakles was fostered by Hera's resentment. His name, in fact, means "Hera's glory."

When Alkmene was about to give birth to Herakles, Zeus, consumed with infatuation for his achievement, proclaimed throughout Olympos that the first male child born on that day was destined to rule. Hera heard this swaggering boast and rushed to Argos, where, she knew, Pelops' daughter Nikippe was also near her time. Hera persuaded the goddess of childbirth, Eleithyia, to hasten the birth of Nikippe's child, called Eurystheus, and to prevent the birth of Herakles. But Eleithyia was tricked by Alkmene's servant girl, and Herakles too was born, although not the first male child of that day. That distinction belonged to Eurystheus, who, because of the proclamation of Zeus and the guile of Hera, was to become ruler of the most powerful city in Argos; Herakles was fated to be subservient to him.

Nonetheless Herakles was destined for greatness. The fabulous exploits that filled his life, as in the case of many heroes, began at infancy. Fearful of Hera's jealous rage, Alkmene sought to destroy the infant Herakles by abandoning him. But the god Hermes brought Herakles to Hera while she slept and put him to her breast. Even as a baby Herakles displayed might and zeal; he nursed so strongly that the goddess, in pain and rage, flung him away, and the milk that continued to flow from her breast formed the constellation known as the Milky Way. Although cruelly rejected by the goddess, Herakles had already drunk enough of the divine milk to insure his immortality and to endow him with a divine strength.

Alkmene and Herakles were reconciled, but Hera sought revenge. Seething with anger and intent on his destruction, the goddess sent two serpents to the crib where he lay sleeping with his half brother, Iphikles, the mortal child of Alkmene. Iphikles merely screamed in fright, but the infant Herakles seized the serpents, one with each hand, and choked them to death.

As a youth, Herakles was instructed in wrestling, archery, and the other manly arts. He was also educated by the wise centaur Cheiron, teacher of Achilles, Jason, and Peleus, and by the famed Linos, son of Apollo, who had introduced the arts of writing and lyre playing to Greece. In one account of Herakles' education, the unfortunate Linos suffered his pupil's fatal blows merely because he had chastised the youth. This violent outburst was the first of many that were to characterize Herakles' behavior. Often he succumbed to fits of rage and indulged in excessive appetites of all kinds; according to one version of his youthful adventures, he impregnated all fifty daughters of King Thespios in one night. By his eighteenth year he was mighty and tall, and it was said that a divine fire burned in his eyes. He roamed the countryside armed only with a giant club made from a huge olive tree that he had pulled out of the ground by its roots.

During one of his youthful travels, Herakles encountered Minyan ambassadors from Orchomenos. They were on their way to Thebes to collect an annual tribute of one hundred cattle from the defenseless Thebans. Herakles cut off their noses and ears and sent the ambassadors back to Orchomenos with these as tribute instead of the cattle. The Minyans, enraged, sent an army against Thebes, but Herakles singlehandedly defeated it and freed Thebes forever from Minyan oppression. King Kreon of Thebes rewarded his valor by giving him his daughter, Megara, in marriage and entrusting him with the government of the city.

For a number of years Herakles lived happily at Thebes, and he had several children by Megara. But his marital bliss was thwarted by Hera, who sent a fit of madness to cloud his senses: unwittingly, he brutally murdered his children. When he recovered and realized the horror of his crime, he left Thebes in despair and sought purification of his blood guilt.

The details of the purification are vague and of little consequence. Rather, the events following it dominated his career. Consulting the Oracle at Delphi for instructions about his future, Herakles was told to live in Tiryns and there to serve Eurystheus, who by now had become king of Mycenae. The Oracle informed him that after he completed a period of servitude, Zeus had promised to grant him immortality.

And now, Eurystheus, fearful of Herakles' strength and growing renown, commanded him to undertake a series of difficult and sometimes mortally dangerous tasks, or *athloi*, which were ultimately intended to bring about his death. These were to become known as the Twelve Labors and form the core of the Herakles myth. There was no consensus in antiquity about either the sequence or the number of the Labors, and many variations of each are known. Moreover, Herakles also performed other heroic deeds, some connected with and some independent of the Labors, and these won him further renown. Those connected with the Labors are known as the *Parerga,* or Works; those independent of the Labors are called the *Praxeis* or Deeds.

The Twelve Labors

The Nemean Lion. Herakles was commanded by Eurystheus to kill a lion sent by Hera to ravage the countryside around Nemea in the Peloponnesos. In some versions of the tale, weapons were useless against the beast, which could be subdued only in a wrestling match. In other accounts, Herakles was able to stun the lion with his great club and dispatch it with his sword. After killing the lion Herakles skinned it and thereafter wore the pelt as his cloak.

The Lernaean Hydra. The Hydra was a hideous, many-headed water snake that wrought havoc on the countryside around Lerna, also in the Peloponnesos. Like the Nemean Lion, the Hydra was reputed to be invincible, for as soon as one head was cut off, two others grew in its stead. To compound the difficulty, Hera sent a giant crab to attack Herakles as he tried to fight the Hydra. Herakles first rid himself of the crab by flinging it into the heavens, where it remained as a constellation. He was then aided by his cousin and faithful companion, Iolaos. As Herakles cut off the heads, Iolaos prevented their monstrous regeneration by searing the wounds with burning stakes. Herakles then further armed himself by dipping his arrows in the Hydra's poisonous blood. Much later, one of these poisonous arrows would cause the death of the wise centaur Cheiron, his former teacher.

The Keryneian Hind. The Third Labor brought Herakles to the high mountains of Arcadia to capture the golden-horned hind, or deer, of Keryneia. This deer ranged the wildest regions of the mountains and lured hunters into hapless pursuit until the hunter himself dropped from exhaustion. For a year Herakles tracked the hind which led him well beyond the boundaries of the world. Finally he was able to overcome it as it swam across a river. He brought it back alive to Mycenae, but not before being stopped by the goddess Artemis, the Huntress, to whom the hind was sacred. Through various means Herakles convinced her that he was under the orders of Eurystheus, and Artemis let him take the hind in peace.

The Erymanthian Boar. Eurystheus ordered Herakles to return to Arcadia to capture the Erymanthian boar, which was devastating the fields in the lower valleys. Herakles drove the creature into deep snow, capturing it there as it floundered, and he returned to Mycenae with his prize.

The Stymphalian Birds. Marshy Lake Stymphalos was inhabited by flocks of enormous birds. These vile creatures, often associated with the Sirens, preyed on men and fouled everything in the area. Herakles frightened them away with a tremendous noise made by a large bronze rattle wrought by the smith god Hephaistos. In other versions of the story, he shot them with his poisonous arrows dipped in the Hydra's blood.

The Augeian Stables. Augeias, king of Elis in the Peloponnesos, kept cattle in stables so filthy that they were the cause of a pestilence that raged throughout the countryside. Eurystheus ordered Herakles to clean them. This task, though not dangerous, was nonetheless a formidable one since Eurystheus required Herakles to execute it in one day. Herakles, greedily eyeing the cattle, privately negotiated with King Augeias for one tenth of the animals in return for clean stables. He then seized the nearby Alpheios and Peneios rivers and, directing them through a hole that he had cut into the foundation of the stables, sluiced them clean in a very short time.

These first six of Herakles' Labors were focused on areas in and around the Peloponnesos, of which Mycenae of the Argolid was one of the major cities. The other six Labors required Herakles to travel further and further from his homeland, and, as one might expect of a hero, to encounter many adventures along the way. In these, the Labors and the Parerga, or Works, begin to mix.

The Horses of Diomedes. For the Seventh Labor, Eurystheus required Herakles to fetch the horses of Diomedes, a Thracian lord who fed them unwary strangers. Herakles managed to seize the cruel Diomedes and throw him to his own horses who, busy with their meal, allowed themselves to be captured.

The Cretan Bull. As the result of a trick that Minos, king of Crete, had played on the god Poseidon, a bull had gone mad and was ravaging the island. Herakles was sent to Crete to capture the bull and bring it back to Eurystheus. Summoning all of his strength, Herakles subdued the beast and, aided by Minos, bound it with a rope. He took it back to Mycenae, where, no longer mad, it was allowed to roam. Eventually the bull wandered to Athens, where it was caught by Theseus and sacrificed to Apollo.

The Amazon's Belt. The land of Pontos, on the Black Sea, was the site of the Ninth Labor. It was there that Herakles, accompanied by a host of comrades, was sent to get the belt of the Amazon queen, Hyppolyte. The belt had been given to her as a sign of her bravery by her father, Ares, god of War. According to some versions of the story, Hyppolyte, who at first was friendly toward Herakles, was inclined to present him with the belt. But at that moment Hera, disguised as an Amazon, went among the Amazon women inciting them to battle with the news that Hyppolyte was being kidnapped by Herakles. The Amazons, wishing to rescue their queen, attacked Herakles and his companions. During the course of the fighting, Herakles killed Hyppolyte and took her belt.

The Cattle of Geryon. The Tenth Labor brought Herakles to the other side of the world to seize the cattle of Geryon, a triple-bodied monster who lived on Erytheia, the island of red sunsets far to the west. Herakles was magically transported to this distant isle in the golden cup of the Sun, which he had commandeered from Helios, the sun god. Geryon's cattle were guarded by the herdsman Eurytion and the two-headed dog Orthos, brother of both the Lernaean Hydra and Kerberos, the hound of Hades. No sooner had Herakles shot and killed Orthos and Eurytion and started to drive away the herd, than Geryon overtook him. But even this adversary was no match for the valor of Herakles. Despite the fact that Geryon fought with three spears and three shields, Herakles shot the monster down with the poisoned arrows and drove the cattle into the golden cup of the Sun. Thus he began his journey back to King Eurystheus. But many obstacles lay in his path as word traveled far that he had seized Geryon's cattle, famed for their beauty. In every city along his route, robbers lay in wait for an opportunity to steal the cattle from Herakles, by now recognized as the most famous cattle thief of them all. The many incidents caused by these brigands during his journey back to Eurystheus form the bulk of the Parerga. Moreover, these encounters provided the basis for an extraordinary genealogy from which every ruling family from North Africa to distant Scythia would claim their descent.

The Apples of the Hesperides. In the Garden of the Hesperides grew a tree that bore golden apples, the objects of Herakles' Eleventh Labor. This wonderful garden was inhabited by three nymphs, daughters of Hesperos, and it lay, like Erytheia, far to the west, at the back of beyond, inaccessible to all but immortals. After some preliminary inquiries, Herakles was directed to Nereus, the Old Man of the Sea, who alone could tell him exactly where the garden was. Nereus turned himself into a variety of forms, including fire and water, in order to escape, but Herakles held fast even to these and finally forced the information from him. However, learning the whereabouts of the garden was only the beginning of the Eleventh Labor. Herakles discovered that in the Garden of the Hesperides the tree that bore the golden fruit was a wedding present to Hera, who had it guarded by a great serpent that never closed its eyes. According to one version of the story, Herakles persuaded the Hesperides to put the serpent to sleep while he plucked the precious apples. In another version Herakles was helped by Atlas, the Titan who supported the earth. Atlas volunteered to get the apples if Herakles would be willing to hold up the world for him in his absence. Herakles, whose strength was boundless, agreed, and the two exchanged places. Atlas soon returned with the apples, but, having experienced freedom from his endless task, insisted that Herakles continue in his stead. Herakles pretended to agree and asked Atlas to hold the Earth for a moment while he fetched a cushion for his shoulders. As soon as Atlas put the apples down and resumed his place, Herakles fled with the golden fruit.

The Hound of Hades. The Twelfth Labor, and by far the most ominous, was the capture of Kerberos, the hound of Hades, god of the Underworld. A number of versions of the story are known, including one in which Herakles had first to be purified of all blood guilt and be initiated into the Eleusinian Mysteries before he could make his descent into the land of the dead. The Underworld was a closed kingdom, never before visited by a living mortal. This was Eurystheus' final attempt to send Herakles to his death. By various forceful means Herakles intruded upon the inviolable realm of Hades where he was tormented by fearsome visions, the shades of heroes who fled from his sight, and various underworld demons. When Herakles finally encountered the hound of Hades, who guarded the gates of the Underworld, it was a frightful sight even to him: a many-headed dog of monstrous size, with snakes growing out of its body, a dog that would devour anyone who tried to escape from this abode of the dead. Tradition records that the hound could be captured only by hand, without the aid of weapons. Herakles, with his superhuman strength, bound the dog to a great chain and thus dragged it into the world of the living. In this fashion Herakles had es-

caped Death for the twelfth time. The way had thus been cleared for him to receive the immortality promised to him by his father, Zeus.

The Parerga, or Works

During these Labors Herakles had been compelled to fight giants and monsters in addition to those directly involved in the Labors. These encounters, known collectively as the Parerga, or Works, are too numerous to recount in detail, but several deserve mention. While Herakles was returning from Erytheia towards the end of the Tenth Labor, the gods were engaged in a hopeless struggle with the giants, monstrous beings representing the primeval forces of the Earth. It had been foretold that victory could be achieved by the gods only with the assistance of a mortal. Zeus called for Herakles, whose presence turned the tide of victory in favor of the gods.

Alkestis, wife of Admetos, king of Pherai in Thessaly, was rescued by Herakles while he was travelling to the court of Diomedes for his Seventh Labor. Alkestis had given her life for that of her husband upon learning that he was incurably ill and that Death was waiting for a victim. Herakles wrestled with Death and forced him to relinquish Alkestis, who was allowed to join her husband, now no longer ill, in the world of the living.

On his way to the Garden of the Hesperides, in the course of his Eleventh Labor, Herakles encountered the giant Antaios, who lived in what is now Libya. Antaios was so strong and skilled in wrestling that he boasted he could build a temple to his father, Poseidon, with the skulls of those he had killed in wrestling matches. Herakles discovered that Antaios' strength came from the Earth, his mother, and that it was renewed each time his foot touched the ground. Herakles exhausted that strength by lifting Antaios up and holding him in the air, and then he squeezed him to death.

While pursuing the Erymanthian boar, Herakles was the guest of the centaur Pholos in his cave. The two were soon attacked by other centaurs, who were attracted by the smell of wine. Herakles killed some and pursued others, by accident mortally wounding Cheiron, his former teacher and beloved friend.

During his Sixth Labor, Herakles had made a bargain with King Augeias for one tenth of the cattle in exchange for his cleaning of the stables. But Augeias went back on his word, claiming that the rivers and not Herakles were responsible for the clean stables. Some time afterward, intent on revenge, Herakles returned to Elis with a host of comrades. He killed King Augeias, ruthlessly ambushed the Molione, twin allies of Augeias, and offered the throne of Elis to Phyleus, Augeias' son and Herakles' benefactor. In celebration of vengeful victory, Herakles founded the Olympic games near Elis in honor of his father, Zeus.

On his return from Erythia with the cattle of Geryon, Herakles came to the Tiber River in Italy at the place where Romulus would eventually found Rome. At that time there lived on the Aventine Hill a terrible fire-breathing, half-human monster called Cacus. Cacus stole the finest of Geryon's cattle and was killed by Herakles for his presumption. Grateful for the recovery of the cattle, Herakles established the Ara Maxima, or Highest Altar, in an area of Rome later to be dedicated to him.

The Praxeis, or Deeds

The Praxeis, or Deeds, make up the third important part of the myth of Herakles. Here, too, the specific episodes are many and often contradictory, in detail as well as in chronology. But the essential elements of the Herakles myth that relate to transgression, retribution, and virtue remain constant. They begin with Herakles' willful murder of Iphitos, the son of the cruel King Eurytos of Oichalia. Although there are conflicting accounts of the episode, all sources agree that Herakles was enamoured of Eurytos' daughter, Iole, and that Herakles received Iphitos at his house with all the hospitality characteristic of the laws of guest friendship, only to murder him treacherously.

The murder of Iphitos required purification and absolution. For this Herakles sought the help of Apollo at his shrine at Delphi. Apollo refused him, whereupon Herakles forced his way into the sacred shrine and tried to steal the holiest of Apollo's cult objects, the sacred tripod cauldron. A struggle between Apollo and Herakles ensued and was halted only by the intervention of Zeus, who, according to some accounts, threw his thunderbolt between the two. Herakles, still stained by the murder of Iphitos, had now compounded his crime by violating the sanctuary of Apollo. Apollo, at the urging of Zeus, finally provided an absolution

—that Herakles be sold into slavery for three years. His purchaser was the Lydian queen, Omphale, who brought him to the East for one of the more bizarre episodes of his life.

At Omphale's court Herakles was required by her to dress in women's clothes and to perform tasks normally carried out by slave girls. In some variations of the story, Herakles and Omphale exchanged clothes, he dressing as a slave girl and she in his lion skin and carrying his club; when he displeased her she would strike him with her sandal. In other accounts, he fathered a son by Omphale; this son was to become ancestor to the founder of the Median dynasty of Persia.

During his servitude to Omphale, Herakles continued to function in a heroic guise by ridding the land of monsters and brigands. Among these were the Kerkopes, strange, monkeylike creatures bent on malicious mischief. While Herakles was sleeping, they attempted to steal his weapons. Awakened suddenly, he captured them, tying each to one end of a pole, intending in this way to bring them to Omphale. But, by their mischief, they incited Herakles to laugh so hard that he set them free.

His servitude to Omphale completed, Herakles was free to resume his life. It may have been during this period that he fought the giant Kyknos and encountered Prometheus, who had just outwitted Zeus. Zeus, in revenge, condemned Prometheus to be tied to a rock, where he was tortured by a vulture who fed perpetually on his liver. Herakles killed the vulture and freed Prometheus.

Herakles also liberated Hesione, daughter of Laomedon, king of Troy. The king had offended Poseidon and was required to make an annual sacrifice of a young virgin to a sea monster. This year the lot fell on Hesione. As she was about to be sacrificed, Herakles appeared. Laomedon promised him his finest horses if Herakles could save her. Herakles slew the monster, but like Augeias, Laomedon went back on his word and incurred Herakles' vengeful wrath. Herakles gathered a host of comrades, took Troy by force, and killed Laomedon.

After a number of other adventures, Herakles met Deianeira, daughter of King Oineus of Kalydon and sister of the hero Meleagros. While in the Underworld, Herakles had encountered Meleagros, who had implored him to marry his still-unwed sister. Oineus stipulated that she could be wed only to the strongest man in the realm. Herakles proved himself to be the only proper suitor, and Deianeira was given to him in marriage. But once again Herakles fell victim to his own rage, when, not realizing his strength, he killed a servant with a blow of his fist. And once again he was compelled to leave his home and purify himself of a blood guilt.

While traveling to the court of Keyx, king of Trachinia, who offered to purify him of the murder of the servant, Herakles and Deianeira encountered the centaur Nessos. Standing at the bank of a river, he offered to carry the young bride across on his back. No sooner had the centaur taken possession of Deianeira than he began to violate her. Herakles, hearing her cries, shot Nessos with one of his poisoned arrows. As the centaur was dying, he performed one last act of treachery: he deceitfully confided to Deianeira that the blood from his wound would have the power to bind Herakles to her in love forever as long as Herakles wore a garment stained with this blood.

According to several of the ancient sources, the killing of the centaur Nessos took place before Herakles' adventure with Iphitos and Iole. Deianeira, left at the court of Keyx while Herakles besieged Oichalia and, later, killed Iphitos, discovered her husband's passion for Iole. When Herakles sent for a sacrificial cloak in order to be properly arrayed for a sacrifice he was about to offer to Zeus on Mt. Oita, Deianeira sought to insure his love for her by sending him his cloak stained with the centaur's blood. As soon as Herakles donned the poisoned cloak, his body began to burn with an unquenchable fire; nor was he able to relieve himself of the poisoned garment. Knowing that his death was at hand, he built himself a funeral pyre and, after giving his bow and quiver to his faithful companion, Philoctetes, begged him to light the fire. But as soon as the pyre began to burn, Zeus sent a cloud from heaven to carry Herakles to the abode of the gods on Olympos. There he was received as an immortal and was reconciled with his bitterest enemy, Hera, who gave her daughter Hebe to him in marriage.

THE HERAKLES MOTIF IN CLASSICAL ART

Religion, myth, and art were closely allied in classical culture in an attempt to give tangible expression to the forces of nature that dominated daily existence. Anthropocentric explanations were invented to account for recurring phenomena, such as seasonal cycles or periodic events, because the forces of the natural world could be comprehended only in terms of human action. The Greek gods, originally conceived as nature divinities, were in themselves less important for an explanation of the cosmos than were the events they caused through their very human emotional outbursts of rage, desire, hatred, and the like. And the half-mortal children of the gods provided the link between divine will and human aspiration. In this context Herakles served to illustrate the consequences of transgression and virtue; and representations of him in art were a constant reminder of these opposing elements of human behavior. Thus the motif of Herakles in his differing roles was woven throughout classical art like an unbroken, multicolored thread whose dominant hue changed according to the need of the age.

The image of Herakles may have appeared in classical art as early as the oldest attempts by Greek artists to represent the human figure. On painted pottery and in small bronzes of the eighth century B.C. of the Geometric Period, one can occasionally find a male figure, nude but for a belt and helmet, who is placed in some deliberate association with a monster recognizable as belonging to the Herakles saga. A small bronze sculpture of a man grappling with a centaur is often taken as a representation of Herakles and the centaur Nessos (Fig. 1), even though centaurs were not limited to the Herakles theme. Here the hero lacks any distinctive identifying attributes other than his nudity and

Fig. 1. *Herakles and the centaur Nessos*. Bronze sculpture. The Metropolitan Museum of Art, Gift of J. Pierpont Morgan. (134447 B)

belt, the standard "dress" of heroes found in Near Eastern art as early as the creation of the Gilgamesh image. The characterization of Herakles in heroic guise was not, however, a consistent feature in Geometric art, where he could also appear as a normal Greek hoplite, or soldier, with spear and shield, identifiable as Herakles only by the presence of some monstrous foe, such as the Lernaean Hydra.

Throughout the course of the seventh century B.C., images of Herakles continued to decorate painted pottery and other objects, but no more frequently than those of other heroes. He did, however, begin to be differentiated from them. Aside from the presence of his adversaries, Herakles was also identified by the special attribute of his club, or an inscription giving his name. By the middle of the seventh century B.C., his iconography and deeds as they appeared on the wood and ivory chest of Kypselos were uniquely his own.

In the sixth century B.C., the Archaic Period, the role of the Herakles motif in Greek art had changed dramatically, and representations of him began to exceed those of any other subject in Archaic art. In addition to his presence in a number of major sculptural decorations for buildings at Delphi, Olympia, and elsewhere, he figured prominently in the architectural sculptures of Athens, where he appeared in nearly all the known pedimental compositions from the middle of the century to the end. Thus he was the focus of the Introduction Pediment, where he is being escorted by Athena into Olympos, symbolized by an oversized seated figure of Zeus (Fig. 2). The so-called Bluebeard Pediment comprised several characters including Triton, an adversary of Herakles invented by Athenian artists around the middle of the century (cf. Cat. Nos. 6 and 10).

Other pedimental groups from the Acropolis preserve both part of the figure of Herakles as he wrestles with the Lernaean Hydra and a second Herakles and Triton ensemble. Toward the end of the sixth century B.C., a large temple on the Acropolis dedicated to Athena was crowned by a sculptural group in the pediment representing a gigantomachy, or battle with the giants. Although this group is known only in isolated figures and fragments, none of which could be identified with Herakles, his presence is nonetheless implied by the assumption in mythology that the gods could conquer the giants only with his assistance.

Much has been said about Herakles' relation to the Athenian tyrant Peisistratos and about the resulting effect on the representations of Herakles in the visual arts of Athens in the second half of the sixth century B.C. Peisistratos may have been the patron who commissioned the many pedimental sculptures featuring Herakles, and some believe that he had adopted the hero as his divine protector. Herakles' close association with Athena, patron goddess of Athens, made him an ideal ally for Peisistratos. Herodotos tells of the entry of the

Fig. 2. *Herakles being escorted by Athena into Olympos.* Introduction Pediment of the Acropolis. Photograph: Deutsches Archäologisches Institut, Athens.

tyrant into Athens, after a brief period of exile, when he was brought up to the Acropolis in a chariot driven by a tall, striking woman dressed as Athena. The populace was deceived into believing that Athena herself was conducting the tyrant into Athens, thereby granting him that special status previously held only by Herakles. Thenceforth, Athena appeared as a standard feature in depictions of Herakles and his Labors, whereas previously she was portrayed in his company only rarely. Vase paintings of the apotheosis of Herakles also became popular at this time, with Athena always included on or near a chariot bearing the hero. Two black-figure vases of the last quarter of the sixth century B.C. (Cat. Nos. 5 and 11) illustrate the consistency with which this motif was represented. The minor variations between the two compositions are due primarily to the increased pictorial area offered by the crater (Cat. No. 11), which enabled the painter to separate the figures of Athena and Herakles.

Other Herakles scenes commonly found in Attic vase painting of the second half of the sixth century B.C. are uncanonical and appear to have no reference in literary sources. Especially unusual is the scene of Herakles being served by Athena. This has no precedent in any of the vase paintings representing episodes from the Herakles cycle, and the scene itself lacks any clear story line. It is known in a series of vases of the end of the sixth century and the beginning of the fifth, among which is the black-figure skyphos (Cat. No. 16). Athena appears in an almost domestic context as she pours wine into a cup held by Herakles, while he raises his hand in a gesture of greeting, or perhaps one signifying "Enough."

This quiet intimacy is in direct contrast to the standard relationship between hero and goddess as it appears in the more orthodox representations on vases from the Herakles cycle, where Herakles is shown engaged in struggle and Athena assists. Typical is the scene with Herakles and the Nemean Lion (Cat. No. 3). Athena passively attends the hero while he subdues the beast; her mere presence is sufficient to assure him victory. While the general compositional scheme is known on scores of vases from this period and may reflect some monumental composition, the somewhat crowded arrangement of the figures and their puppet-like movements are characteristic of the work of the Swing Painter, an anonymous craftsman to whom dozens of Herakles scenes have been

attributed. His style, generally reflective of trends in the third quarter of the sixth century, is in marked contrast to a later sixth century representation of Herakles battling the giant Kyknos (Cat. No. 17). Here Athena, no longer a passive observer, appears to rush toward the other side of the vase brandishing her spear, while on the opposite panel Herakles lunges forward, about to thrust his spear through the fallen body of the giant. The dynamic action and bold postures of the figures, as well as the daring foreshortening of the shield and the frontal foot of the giant, are characteristics often found in Late Archaic painting as the artists became more proficient in the depiction of the human body in movement.

In the monumental arts of the fifth century B.C., the Classical Period, the image of Herakles more than that of any other hero continued to be found among the major architectural sculptures, although not nearly as frequently as in the sixth century. A full cycle of his Labors comprises the metopes of the early classical temple of Zeus at Olympia, and later, in the fifth century, the same theme decorated the metopes of the Hephaisteion at Athens. A relief on the Altar of the Twelve Gods in Athens portrayed Herakles among other heroes as a reminder of the god's blessings on the virtuous. He was included on the east metopes and in the east pediment of the Parthenon, and in the gigantomachy on the inside face of the shield of Athena Parthenos, the cult statue for the Parthenon. Elsewhere around the Greek world he made sporadic appearances in other gigantomachies, amazonomachies, and trojanomachies.

Moreover, we are told by ancient writers that the early fifth-century sculptor Myron made several free-standing statues of Herakles, none of which has survived, although one of them may be reflected in a Roman marble statuette now in the Museum of Fine Arts in Boston. Myron also made a statue group of Athena, Herakles, and Zeus for the sanctuary of Hera on Samos. Onatas of Aegina crafted a bronze statue of Herakles for the Thasians at Olympia that was admired by many, as was the colossal relief of Athena and Herakles which the later fifth century sculptor Alkamenes made for the sanctuary of Herakles at Thebes.

But in spite of these major compositions and large scale sculptures, the focus on Herakles' exploits was less emphatic in the Classical Period than it was in the Archaic, especially in vase painting. For the Greeks of the Classical Period, with their strong moral and ethical codes of behavior, Herakles' expansive and rather defiant character, and his propensity for fits of rage and almost unbridled violence, were excessive. Nor were these characterizations compatible with the quest for an understanding of the nature of man that had emerged in Greek philosophical thought. New types of Herakles were developed and existed alongside the old. The fifth-century poet Pindar abhorred the violence and seeming lawlessness of Herakles, yet he held him up as the model of virtue to which all athletes should aspire. For Pindar, the labors of Herakles had come to indicate greatness of spirit and a passion for justice and order; it was these attributes, rather than his physical strength, that Pindar advised young men to emulate. In this period Herakles also began to be seen as a tragic figure, one who was unjustly persecuted and who suffered emotional as well as physical stress.

One of the best visual indications of these changes is seen in the metope from the temple of Zeus at Olympia showing Herakles and the Nemean Lion (Fig. 3). In the metope, Herakles, hardly more than an adolescent, is shown completely exhausted from his extraordinary toil as he leans, head in hand, over the lion; Athena attends him with quiet concern. This motif is repeated almost identically in a small

Fig. 3. *Herakles and the Nemean Lion.* Metope at Olympia. Photograph: Deutsches Archäologisches Institut, Athens.

bronze statuette that once decorated an Etruscan candelabrum (Cat. No. 29). The difference in the conception of the heroic struggle between the Swing Painter's amphora of the sixth century (Cat. No. 3) and the Olympia metope is vast. In the metope there is a strong psychological content as a young Herakles, already totally exhausted, contemplates not only the deed accomplished but the immensity of those yet to be performed.

The choice of a meaningful moment in the representation of a scene, such as on the Olympia metope, was also made by the vase painters of the fifth century B.C. Canonical motifs of the type developed in Peisistratid Athens were still produced, as is seen on the black-figure lekythos, or oil jug, with Herakles and the Cretan Bull, dating around 475 B.C. (Cat. No. 19). However, there began to appear completely unconventional episodes and a focus on pivotal acts not necessarily crucial to the epic character of the narrative. By the association of deeds and consequences, the viewer well versed in myth and legend could be prompted to recall all that went before and, in the case of the Olympia metope, all that was to come in a given story. A red-figure psykter, or wine cooler, from the middle of the fifth century depicts Herakles on his funeral pyre on Mt. Oita, handing over his divine bow to Philoctetes (Fig. 4). Just as Herakles had released Prometheus from his suffering, so did Philoctetes, by lighting the pyre, release Herakles from the torment inflicted on him by the centaur Nessos' treachery and his wife Deianeira's jealousy. The viewer would recognize that the essential moment of Herakles' apotheosis was imminent, even if the participants in the actual drama do not. The viewer would also remember all the trials and suffering that led up to this moment of salvation. We need not have been shown a heroic encounter to recognize in the finely drawn youthful perfection of the figure of Herakles the embodiment of the heroic ideal as extolled by Pindar.

The fourth century B.C., or Late Classical Period, was a period of adjustment and reassessment for the classical mind. The high ideals of the fifth century were betrayed by the personal ambitions of a few who were the catalysts for the disasters that collectively made up the Peloponnesian War. The moral disillusionment and spiritual exhaustion brought about by the war made a strong impact on the art of the period, which increasingly focused on the personal and emotional content inherent in a subject. Herakles' suffering and his persecution by Hera were exploited for their symbolic value as a didactic expression of the human condition in which there is transgression, guilt, and retribution. But in spite of human imperfection, a just reward is promised to those who can endure.

Fig. 4. *Herakles' funeral pyre on Mt. Oita.* Attic red figure psykter. Malcolm Weiner Collection, New York.

A number of artists of the fourth century contributed their own characterizations of Herakles. These included the sculptors Scopas of Paros and a certain Praxiteles, who was said to have sculpted a pedimental group for the temple of Herakles at Thebes, and the painters Zeuxis and Apelles. But by far the single most impressive and influential contribution to the development of the Herakles motif came from Lysippos of Sikyon, a sculptor working in the latter half of the fourth century B.C. It was his innovative spirit that is generally recognized as opening the first act on the Hellenistic Age (323–31 B.C.). Of the fifteen hundred works that are traditionally ascribed to him by ancient writers, his various sculptures

of Herakles won him the most renown and were the start of an enormous artistic progeny reaching not only through the Hellenistic and Roman Imperial eras, but into the Middle Ages, the Renaissance and beyond.

The most important of his Herakles sculptures was an overly muscular representation of the hero leaning on his club as a support; his left arm hung down limply while his right hand was behind his back holding the Apples of the Hesperides. This last element indicated the completion of Herakles' Labors and reminded the viewer of what was interpreted in the fourth century as the extraordinary suffering and toil that he had endured. Called the Weary Herakles, the statue is best known from the Roman copy once in the Farnese collection and signed by the copyist Glykon of Athens. Even though the motif of a male figure leaning on a support was not invented by Lysippos, he gave it new meaning in its contrast of superhuman strength and the total vulnerability implied by the limp fall of the arm over the club. As a symbol of human suffering and salvation, its appeal in Hellenistic and Roman art was enormous, and copies and free adaptations were made in all media for centuries after it was created (Cat. Nos. 41 and 42). It even became the emblem of cities and emperors, appearing as a device on state or imperial coinage. Each one of the copies of the Weary Herakles was touched in some way by the style or predilection of the copyist. A head belonging to a late Hellenistic or early Roman Imperial version (Cat. No. 39) retains the rich modeling of the face characteristic of the mature work of Lysippos, but it betrays its late Hellenistic date in the almost monotonous stylization of the locks of the hair, which are more in keeping with the classical revival of the first century B.C.

A second Herakles type has also been ascribed to Lysippos. According to tradition he made a statuette of a seated Herakles to grace the table of Alexander the Great. Known as the Herakles Epitrapezios, meaning "on the table," its fame inspired hundreds of copies and variations (Cat. Nos. 35 and 43). Both Statius and Martial marveled at the paradox of such great strength and monumentality portrayed in so small a scale. We can perhaps see a glimpse of this quality in a Roman marble copy of this famous statuette (Cat. No. 43). The energetic posture of Herakles, leaning back, turning his head towards the right, is filled with a restlessness conveyed through the contrast of the open pose and the constriction of the well-developed muscle of the torso.

Lysippos also created, for the city of Taranto, a colossal statue of a seated Herakles, best known through a partially-preserved Roman copy called the Torso Belvedere. For the city of Alyzia in Akarnania he also made a sculptural group of Herakles' Labors. The individual motifs from this group are perhaps reflected in the miniature reliefs representing the Labors found on a jeweler's core of the second century B.C. (Cat. No. 34).

Alexander the Great (355-323 B.C.), king of Macedonia and Lord of Asia, had a special veneration for Herakles as Phylakos, or guardian, of the Macedonian dynasty. Lysippos, as court artist to Alexander, sculpted a portrait head of Alexander wearing the Nemean lion skin cap. This head has a distinctive stylistic relationship to a Herakles head on tetradrachms, or four drachma coins, minted by Alexander and produced posthumously for a number of decades (Cat. No. 24). Both heads reflect the concept of an ideal prince of youthful perfection rather than that of a violent strongman. In fourth century philosophy Herakles became the paradigm for *arete*, or virtue, and a model of action. Representations of Alexander with the attributes of Herakles presented him as the living embodiment of the hero who, through virtue and just behavior, brought order to the known world. The rich sculptural modulation of the face on the tetradrachm incites a surface movement that marks the face with a radiant energy. This quality was said to have been characteristic of Alexander himself and was one that, according to Plutarch, Lysippos alone among artists could capture.

Even though earlier rulers may have utilized the Herakles motif for political advantage, as we have seen with Peisistratos in archaic Athens, Alexander gave his association with Herakles a new meaning as the two personalities began to merge into one and a unique closeness was established between mortal ruler and divine hero. Eventually, to the successors of Alexander, Herakles as the object of a hero cult became second in importance to the concept of a hero ruler.

For the artists of the Hellenistic Age (323-31 B.C.) the slim and youthful Herakles type created by Lysippos for Alexander was far less popular than the Weary Herakles conception of the hero, brawny and perhaps a little obtuse. While no new types of Herakles developed in the Hellenistic Age, different attitudes toward him resulted in the creation of satirical or playful images that were far from the concept of manly virtue displayed in the Alexander-Herakles images and touted in the Classical Period. Innumerable were the motifs that developed once Lysippos opened the door on the paradox of muscular strength and human weakness. Herakles' excesses were seen as leading to humiliation. He was often portrayed drunk or suffering from the side-effects of too much drink. A bronze statuette, conceived stylistically in the manner of the Weary Herakles, shows Herakles reeling backward, laboring in this instance not for some virtuous end, but merely to keep himself erect. A well-known theme was that of Herakles urinating, another illustration of the effects of overindulgence this type of sculpture was popular for fountain sculptures, especially in Roman gardens of the early Imperial Era. Or, in yet other representations, Herakles, having fallen asleep in a drunken stupor, was shown victimized by tiny, playful Erotes, who steal his wine as well as his club (Fig. 5). The contrast between brutish behavior and innocent playfulness is epitomized on a bronze applique (Cat. No. 33). Here a boyish Eros, his long hair tied at the top of his head in a knot and held in place by the jaw of the Nemean Lion skin, parodies the strongman image of Herakles.

Herakles motifs were also frequently used in the decorative arts of the Hellenistic Era where the fullest ornamental value could be realized from the repetitive patterns of Herakles' hair. the beard and the lion skin. A frontal face of Herakles served as an embellishment for the handle attachment of a situla, or bucket (Cat. No. 25). Here a striking decorative effect was achieved by using movement directed outward from the central axis of the face through a series of undulating lines, in mirror image to one another, in the beard and lion skin. The patterns realized through the contrast of light and shadow result in an almost baroque richness for the object, which would have been set off all the more by the plain surface of the situla it once ornamented. Thus the Herakles motif in the Hellenistic Era came to be regarded also as a vehicle for ornament and for frivolity, partly because of its decorative potential and partly because of the ribald subject matter that could be gleaned from the less than virtuous behavior of the hero.

The Herakles motif was used with great reverence, however, by the Etruscans of central Italy for whom Herakles was a major living force. Known epigraphically as Hercle, or Herecle, Herakles' name was invoked by the Etruscans for protection not only for themselves but also for springs, mountains, streams, and gateways. His image frequently decorated the pediments of Etruscan temples, stood over their gables, and appeared as a badge of protection on coins from city mints. He was the most frequently represented hero in Etruscan art.

Fig. 5. *Herakles recumbent*. Marble relief. Bowdoin College Museum of Art, Gift of Edward Perry Warren. (1906.2)

Along with the cult of Apollo, that of Herakles achieved a primary position in Etruscan religious practices, although the exact nature of his cult still remains vague. Hundreds of bronze statuettes of him were found in the many sanctuaries and shrines bearing his name and must have been offered as part of religious ritual or as thank-offerings. The earliest appearance of these votive bronzes was in the sixth century B.C., but their popularity significantly increased in the fourth century and later. Several different types were known. The most common was the attacking, beardless Herakles wearing the lion skin as a helmet and wielding his club. Cat. Nos. 28, 30, and 31 present three variations on this theme. The somewhat stunted proportions and oversized heads of these statuettes are typical of Etruscan small-scale sculpture of the late fourth and third centuries B.C. Never intended to be examples of high art, these statuettes perhaps illustrate the more commonplace style indigenous to any folk tradition. This tradition was so strong that, by the end of the Hellenistic Era, this Etruscan type of Herakles became the basis for the single most popular votive statuette in Roman Gaul, Italy, and Spain (Cat. No. 47).

But alongside this folk tradition, with its inconsistencies in proportion, is a rather fine, large statuette of Herakles standing at rest (Cat. No. 32). The more elegant proportions seen here are based on a closer observation of the canons of Greek sculpture, and the idealized face, with its large, thickly lidded eyes and barest hint of pathos, recalls one of the Lysippan portraits of Alexander.

For the people who settled on the hills to the side of the Tiber River, in what eventually became Rome, Herakles was one of the most venerated gods. His name was Latinized to Hercules, but his image and myth remained essentially Greek. By the second century B.C., when the Romans first recognized the need for an artistic expression for their religious beliefs, Roman artists were content to use for their representations of Herakles the Lysippan Herakles types that were readily available for study and reproduction. The Romans admired and avidly collected Greek works of art, either out of concern for their preservation, as was the case with Lysippos' Alyzia group of the Labors of Herakles or, more normally, as loot from conquered cities to be displayed in triumph. By the beginning of the

first century B.C., the Capitoline Hill in Rome and its surrounding area were full of Greek monuments dedicated to Hercules, including the Tarentine colossus of Lysippos, the first true Greek work of art to be brought to Rome. Because of Herakles' victories over his adversaries, he was linked to triumphs, and offerings were made to him of a percentage of the spoils of war. In fact, the entire Capitoline area had a triumphal character. Here Hercules was worshipped as Invictus, or invincible, in the many sanctuaries, including the Ara Maxima Herculis, or Highest Altar of Hercules. According to Roman tradition, this altar was founded by Herakles himself on the occasion of his defeat of the monster Cacus, who lived in what had become Rome.

Hercules was widely worshipped also around the countryside outside Rome, as well as in every other Roman city or town, where gymnasiums, theaters, and other public buildings bore his name. Most of the time the representation of Hercules followed Greek, if not Lysippan, models. A short distance from Rome, at Alba Fucens, an important sanctuary to Hercules had been renovated toward the end of the second century B.C. In general format it followed the Greek model of the four-columned shrine that was typical for hero cults, and it contained a colossal version of the Herakles Epitrapezios by Lysippos for a cult statue.

Other well-known Lysippan types of Herakles were used as motifs in the elaborate mythological paintings that decorated the walls of Roman houses and public buildings. A well-known scene of Herakles discovering his infant son Telephos was painted in the basilica at Herculaneum in the first century A.D. and included a depiction of Herakles that closely followed the pose of the Weary Herakles by Lysippos, although here it was seen from the rear. Elsewhere, at Pompeii, the Tarentine Herakles was part of a composition showing Orpheus and the Muses. In both instances, Herakles was painted in dark tones against a generally light background, as if to suggest that the model for the figure was a bronze sculpture.

The opportunity to utilize the Herakles motif for political purposes was not ignored by the Romans. While many aristocrats identified with him (Cat. No. 40) and images of Alexander-Herakles as the ideal ruler continued to be made (Cat. No. 51), a few Roman emperors actually presented themselves as the living Hercules (Cat. No. 46). What may have begun as a superstitious belief among the peoples of Near Asia subjugated by Alexander that he and Herakles were one became, in the megalomaniac personalities of several emperors of the second and third centuries A.D., the actual conviction that they were the incarnation of the divine hero on earth. The most infamous of these was Commodus, whose lunacy drove him to dress in nothing but Herakles' lion skin and pantomime the Labors in front of audiences in the amphitheater, using live beasts and gladiators as his adversaries. Commodus' interest in Herakles stemmed less from a desire to present himself in the guise of the champion of order than from a passion for athletic games. A portrait bust of the emperor, endowed with his specific, although slightly idealized, features, represented him wearing the lion skin of Herakles over his elaborately curled hair and holding the club in one hand and the Apples of the Hesperides in the other.

The incongruity of an image that contains references to a divine and mythological personality, on the one hand, and yet has the temporal quality of specific portrait features, on the other, was often found in Roman portrait sculpture. Perhaps the most amusing example of this concerning Herakles is a portrait of a middle-aged Roman woman with a careful and stylish coiffure, shockingly nude but for Herakles' lion skin and club. In this instance the reference was to Omphale, the Lydian queen who held Herakles in servitude and who compelled him to wear the clothes of a woman while she assumed his attributes of power, the club and lion skin.

Having a woman assume the attributes of Herakles was entirely novel in Roman art. It became somewhat popular in the second and third centuries A.D., where we can find the Omphale motif used to decorate a sarcophagus surely made for a woman (Cat. No. 54), or used indirectly and discreetly, with a touch of humor, by a goldsmith who fashioned earrings in the form of a tiny Herakles club (Cat. No. 52).

Yet the worship of Hercules in the Roman Empire was essentially a deeply spiritual one for the majority of the populace. His worship not only offered the promise of divine protection but also held out hope for a life beyond death. Herakles' descent into the Underworld associated him with Orpheus, another Greek hero around whose worship were assembled the mysteries of nature and a hope for resurrection. The emphasis on a mystical element in the Hercules cult that developed in the later second and third centuries A.D. may have been in response to a need for a more personal religious experience as the mechanisms of state government and state religion fell into disorder. Not only did Herakles, through his Labors, bring order into a chaotic world once inhabited by monsters and brigands, but also the cycle of his suffering and redemption in his Labors and apotheosis illustrated philosophical concepts regarding the nature of the soul. The Neo-Platonic philosopher Plotinus, living in the mid third century A.D., wrote in his *Enneads* (I, xii), "It is a universally admitted belief that the soul commits sins, expiates them, undergoes punishment in the visible world and passes into new bodies." In these contexts, the Twelve Labors became popular again after many centuries of relative neglect. They were often depicted in sarcophagi or funerary painting, and many are the independent scenes from a cycle of Labors that now exist in a fragmentary state, or separated from their original contexts. A single bronze plaque from the later fourth century A.D., certainly once part of a set of twelve, depicts Herakles and the Lernaean Hydra (Cat. No. 56). The complicated pose of the hero, with his foreshortened leg thrust into one of the great coils of the monster, and the passive expression of his face dominated by large, round eyes, illustrate the classical revival of the fourth century that accompanied the consolidation of the Roman Empire under Constantine the Great. Yet the classical vocabulary of posture and expression was already disintegrating in the face of rich linear flourishes that stressed the decorative aspect of the image rather than the narrative. Moreover, the contrasting patterns of color achieved through the use of various inlaid metals served to heighten the overall decorative effect.

The advent of Christianity and the development of Christian dogma through the second and third centuries A.D. furnished still further motivation for an emphasis on the Herakles motif. In this instance, like Dionysos and Apollo, who served as Christ images, references to Herakles could be used to disguise the Christian message of salvation and resurrection from the pagan Roman persecutors of the Christian faith. With the Peace of the Church in A.D. 313 and the establishment of Christianity as the state religion, the motif of Herakles' Labors continued to prosper, not only on sarcophagi but in all aspects of the decorative arts, in silver plate, glass vessels, reliquaries, caskets, and in textiles. The last are particularly well known from the site of Coptos in Egypt, then part of the Roman empire, where a strong classical tradition lingered as late as the sixth century A.D., although in a very provincial style. Cat. No. 61 is an embroidered panel from a sixth-century funerary shroud. It is decorated with a full, although uncanonical, series of Herakles' Labors surrounding a Dionysiac motif and again speaks of the joys of salvation achieved through suffering. The arrangement and content of the Labors on this panel are identical to several others known to be from Coptos and may have been copied from some well-known Herakles cycle circulated through pattern books. The Coptic style illustrated by the rather blocky and disjointed, although spirited, figures relies on the decorative contrasts of eccentric shapes rather than on any attempt to create a coherent figure. This style is also evident in stone carving, such as the relief with Herakles and the Cretan Bull (Cat. No. 57), perhaps a fragment of a cycle from a larger architectural decoration. Here the deep undercutting and extravagant use of the drill create the same stark contrast of dark against light seen in the shroud panel.

The disintegration of classical form evident in Coptic art and represented by these two works was not universally felt throughout the Roman Empire of the sixth century A.D. Elsewhere the century saw the first major classical revival of the Byzantine Era. Nor did the Herakles motif languish, as the hero now continued to stand as the model of virtue, strength, and salvation through suffering throughout the postclassical civilizations of the Mediterranean and Europe.

Meanwhile, beyond the immediate confines of the classical world of Greece, Etruria, and Rome, the Herakles motif also played an important role. In the ancient Near East he was the most popular figure from Greek mythology, as can be documented in the art of Cyprus, Syria, Mesopotamia, Iran, and Afghanistan, where he was assimilated with local sky gods and with a lion-wrestling hero (Cat. No. 59) who ultimately goes back to the Bronze Age Gilgamesh.

Cyprus is at the crossroads between Greece and Asia and, as such, received cultural stimuli from both. The cult of Melkart, a sky god of the Semitic pantheon, was brought by the Phoenicians to Cyprus where, under reciprocal Greek influence, it was fused with the cult of Herakles. Hundreds of votive statuettes in limestone and terracotta testify to the popularity of Herakles-Melkart from the end of the sixth century B.C. through the Roman Imperial Era, especially in the sanctuaries of Resef-Apollo. The motif of Herakles appeared as a device on the coins of Kition and Salamis even more frequently than that of the Aphrodite of Cyprus, called the Cyprian. In the Hellenistic Era, the image of Herakles was augmented with a cornucopia as he became a god of peace and the source of good fortune and plenty.

A large limestone statuette of a youthful Herakles wearing the lion skin illustrates the Herakles-Melkart type of the early fifth century B.C. (Cat. No. 20). The rigid frontality, the broad, simplified surfaces, and the emphatic linear detail of the figure are characteristics assimilated into Cypriote sculpture from the artistic conventions of Syria and Egypt. Only the square face with its heavy jaw and hint of a smile betrays true Greek stylistic conventions.

Even more eastern in appearance is a relief from a base once supporting a colossal statue of Herakles-Melkart of the later sixth century B.C. Arranged in horizontal registers is a lively narrative representation of Herakles stealing the cattle of Geryon (Cat. No. 7). The low, flat relief technique and the extreme linear stylization of the figures are reminiscent of Egyptian tomb reliefs and Assyrian hunting reliefs of the eight and seventh centuries B.C.

Even though the Herakles motif was assimilated into Cypriote art as early as the sixth century B.C., it was not until the late fourth century B.C. that it can be documented in the Near East, and only in the second century A.D. that it became popular. The cult of Herakles was particularly well established at Dura-Europos, a provincial site in Syria where many relief representations of Herakles were found. Cat. No. 58 is typical of the Syrian conception of Herakles as it appeared in household shrines at Dura, where the hero seems to have been worshipped as a household diety. The relief, executed in the coarse but expressive provincial style of Syria of the fourth century A.D., confronts the viewer with the insistence on hieratic frontality so characteristic of ancient Near Eastern cult images.

Evidence indicates that the worship of Herakles had travelled with Alexander and his army in their drive eastward into central Asia, where soldier's graffiti and crude reliefs record the need for Herakles' protection in a strange and hostile land. First the Bactrians and then the Parthians, living in what is now Iran and Afghanistan, accepted Herakles into their worship, as did the Kushans, who lived further to the East, particularly in the first few centuries of our era. Representations of Herakles are known in the Ghandaran art of India, where he appears perhaps as Vasudeva, last sovereign of the early Kushan dynasty, or in association with the Indian god Siva. The head of a man wearing a lion skin cap (Cat. No. 60) is stylistically associated with Gandharan art of the fifth century A.D. and relates to the stucco heads that served as architectural decoration at Haḍḍa and other sites in Peshawar in northwest Pakistan. Yet the iconography, so strongly and uniquely Herakles', links this work from the easternmost frontier of the Late Antique world with all those from Greece, Etruria, and Rome; this link illustrates the overwhelming importance and persistence of the Herakles motif in classical antiquity.

HERAKLES IN GREEK
AND ROMAN MYTHOLOGY

Every age needs heroes and symbolic figures to embody its ideals and emotions. In our age, with its penchant for psychological affliction, Oedipus, Narcissus, and Sisyphus may be congenial, and Herakles once more seems to be relegated to a one-dimensional role as a paragon of superhuman physical strength.

Such, however, was not his fate in either Greco-Roman antiquity nor in the mythological and artistic traditions that followed well into the twentieth century. There the range of his roles and characterizations far surpasses that of any other mythological figure. We see him, often simultaneously, as a great tragic sufferer and as a comic, lecherous, and gluttonous monster, as a metaphysical struggler and romantic (or not so romantic) lover, as an exemplar of virtue and an embodiment of incredible, purely physical strength, as a divine mediator, and as the incarnation of rhetoric, intelligence, and wisdom. The contradictory nature of his qualities allowed for ever new modifications and the creative exploitation of their inherent tensions.

It is true that mythological characters evolve, but not in a linear and progressive way. Indeed the full and complex range of Herakles' many qualities is never present in any single portrait, literary or artistic, nor in a single locale. He became many different things to many different men, and while it is useful to categorize his roles and adaptations, we should not do so in the spirit of Procrustes. And we must realize that during classical antiquity, no version of a given myth ever became canonical. Instead, myth remained alive because of its changeability, and the constant inventive additions to any myth were a sign of its strength and adaptability.

The origins of the Greek Herakles lay probably in the folktale in which he was the type of strong boy who recurs, with a different ethnicity, as Jack the Giant-killer, der starke Hans, Juan de l'Os or Giovanni Benforte. The essential change in Herakles' historical development from folktale to myth came when he entered into the world of cult and his existence assumed a spiritual as well as a timelessly entertaining dimension. When and where this took place is impossible to ascertain; besides, the Greeks were notoriously unconcerned about a systematic chronology of myth. Given Herakles' strong association with Tiryns and Thebes, however, it is reasonable to assume that he already figured prominently in the Mycenaean heroic age of myth which left its important legacy for later Greece. Tiryns was a vassal town of Mycenae; Herakles thus became the vassal of Eurystheus, the legendary king of Mycenae who supervised, perhaps with some trepidation, Herakles' various labors (which, incidentally, always numbered more than twelve).

What distinguishes Herakles from other mythological heroes is that he belonged to all of Greece and became the one true panhellenic hero. It is a misconception that he was merely the property of the Dorians, into whose genealogy he was, in fact, fitted rather indirectly. His cult and shrines were found all over Greece, Attica being a splendid example. As a hero in myth and cult, Herakles replaced, in many towns, local heroes and even gods whose exploits were promptly absorbed into his grander mythology. Because he was the national hero of Greece, all kinds of characteristics were attributed or transferred to him. His myth absorbed them with the same dispatch with which Herakles completed even his most difficult labors. Herakles was thus a composite hero who arose from a confluence and diversity of traditions.

A second phenomenon, peculiar only to Herakles in the pantheon of Greek mythology, was that his cult in Greece was dual: he was worshipped as both a hero and a god—the "hero god," as Pindar called him. Even though the line between hero and god was not always sharply drawn, especially in Greek literature, the basic distinction between the two was well known. In contrast to the god, the hero was originally a man who came to enjoy divine honors only after his death, usually because he deserved well of his society or mankind in general. Plausibility and the literary evidence overwhelmingly support the view that Herakles first was man, then a hero, and then also became a god, rather than the other way around. The great German scholar Wilamowitz, therefore, was essentially correct in summing up the essence of Herakles by saying: "He was born man, became god; suffered labors and gained heaven." It was a dynamic ideal that struck a resonant chord in the Greeks'—and all of mankind's—longing for immortality, which is the guiding theme even of the earliest work of Greek literature, Homer's *Iliad.* Since it was also a profoundly personal and individual ideal, it preserved its timelessness well throughout the Roman period; in due course, Dante and others could consider Herakles as a proto-Christ.

Still, the semi-divine descent of Herakles is not given much emphasis in literature and art. He was, after all, the son of Zeus, a distinction which did not amount to anything strikingly unique among the mythological population of Greece. The one trait which is common to the Herakles of all periods and was enhanced by his divine parentage is his more than human strength and endurance. On a primitive level, it operates in purely physical terms and, therefore, like most human qualities, is rather ambivalent. It can be used for a bad purpose, with terrifying results: this is the Herakles who kills a host in a fit of rage, who ransacks a house to heap up a pyre for his children, who kills his wife in a frenzy, or deflowers and impregnates fifty girls in one night. "Nothing in excess" may have been a noble motto, but conformance to it would relegate mythological heroes quickly to the non-mythological world of convention and boredom.

Moreover, while some authors and artists developed the negative implications of Herakles' superhuman strength, the other, predominant part of the tradition emphasized Herakles' use of it for his personal or, more frequently yet, the common good. This had its basis in cult: all over Greece Herakles was commonly worshipped as *alexikakos,* averter of evil, which was understood in its broadest sense: war, death, ghosts, sickness, indeed, all of life's trials and tribulations. Herakles was not a remote and ultimately irrelevant figure, like some of the Olympians; the common man called upon him as a trustworthy and invincible divine helper against all evils. From this source, too, springs Herakles' important role as a culture hero. He could rid the world of monsters and protect and preserve human society from its natural enemies. These labors and exploits, of course, furnished vase painters and sculptors with a wealth of material.

Herakles' role expanded to the territories which the Greeks colonized or were trying to colonize. He became the embodiment of Greek civilization facing barbarians such as king Busiris of Egypt, who, like Cyclops in the *Odyssey,* flouted the obligations of guest friendship and murdered strangers at the altar. Besides, the purpose of Greek mythology was always hellenocentric: faraway places would be brought into the orbit of Greek civilization by being given a connection with a Greek hero. This mythological linkage with Herakles was especially strong in Sicily and southern Italy.

The versatility of Herakles in all these respects was enhanced by both unparalleled popularity on the comic stage and his recurrence in the works of Euripides, Prodicus, and the Stoics. No other character was as popular in Greek comedy because, being bigger than life to begin with, he provided so much opportunity for mayhem and the sort of exaggeration on which comedy flourishes. The vase paintings from southern Italy in particular bear eloquent testimony to this. This was not a sign of disrespect; Herakles was the most popular figure in the ancient "festive" comedy precisely because the Greeks took him seriously, more seriously, at any rate, than other deities. At the same time, Euripides portrayed Herakles as the supreme example of a man achieving heroism of a grandeur which even the gods cannot attain, precisely because they are not human. Finally, Prodicus elevated Herakles to being the protagonist in his allegory of the choice between Virtue and Vice, which was to have a powerful impact, especially on the Renaissance.

Two related developments took place in Hellenistic times, which also left their mark on Herakles' acceptance in Rome. One is Alexander the Great's emulation of the hero. The lion's skin became part of his iconography and it was not an irrelevant detail: like Herakles, Alexander's mission was to be a culture hero to foreign lands, and there was the implication—and often more than that—of divinity. Secondly, the Stoics found in Herakles an embodiment of their acceptance of divine will and of their tenets of endurance and austerity. The Herakles Farnese of the fourth century is a splendid sculptural expression of the same ethic.

Rome's contributions to the development of the Herakles myth did not lie in the realm of mythopoeia. Instead, Herakles was a religious figure, and this profoundly influenced his characterization in Roman literature and art. While he had been the one panhellenic hero, he was also immensely popular in Italy. "One could scarcely find a place in Italy in which the god is not honored," wrote one of the most knowledgeable observers of Rome, Dionysios of Halikarnassos, in his *Roman Antiquities*. This popularity, which is documented in Etruscan art, too, was not imposed on the populace from above (as was, for instance, the legend of Aeneas before Vergil gave it a truly popular basis, probably because he linked it with the Herakles myth). Rather, especially in Rome, Herakles satisfied true religious longings which the ritualistic and rather impersonal state religion could not fulfill.

The essential characteristic of the Roman Hercules cult was its freedom from the calcification of the pontifical religion. His worship remained private and individual, in contrast to the traditional gods of the state religion: Herakles was worshipped on individual occasions rather than one day of the year; the people—rather than the priests alone—partook in the sacrificial banquet; and far from being localized at one, state-supported sanctuary, Herakles' cult was practised in a multitude of smaller shrines and temples which had been built as tokens of private gratitude. He satisfied the personal religious needs that were left unfulfilled by the state religion and,

therefore, came to share in the same religious intensity which the oriental cults enjoyed for precisely the same reason. The capacities in which he was invoked ranged from ensurer of an easy birth to silent partner in business deals. In short, while these are similar to the functions of *alexikakos* he had in Greece, the difference is that he was viewed in Rome almost entirely as a patron saint who would help one overcome all imaginable difficulties in life. Herakles thus became Hercules *invictus*, the invincible one. And, as had been the case with Alexander, Roman generals from Scipio to Mark Antony identified with him as a role model as did, in a more debased way, later emperors such as Commodus.

In sum, as one scholar put it quite aptly, in passing from Greece to Rome Herakles took on a new seriousness more in keeping with the character of the people who welcomed him. There was a spiritual affinity between this hero and the Roman psyche because the ability to endure and the persistence in undertaking troublesome labors were not abstract, philosophical virtues for the Romans, but national characteristics. Furthermore, corresponding to the strong social ethic of the Romans, Herakles' heroism was always *pro bono publico*; he incurred his toils and labor as he was pursuing goals and a mission set by the gods, Jupiter in particular. For good reason, then, the poets would associate him prominently with a good emperor such as Augustus.

Since Roman religion, in contrast to the Greek, was not mythopoeic, little was added to the Herakles myth in terms of new stories or adventures. The principal exception is his founding of the Ara Maxima in Rome, where he slew the monster Cacus and thereby made the site of Rome safe for civilization; the event even preceded Rome's actual founding by Romulus. The importance of Rome's contribution to the Herakles myth lay not in more mythmaking, but in the spiritual aspect of more seriousness and *gravitas*. Roman religion and the philosophies, predominantly Stoicism—and the Romans were Stoics long before Stoicism became a philosophical system—worked hand in hand to shape an image of the hero whose *gravitas* has been a distinctive trait to our day. Along with the breadth of his activities and characteristics, this *gravitas* assured him a preeminent place in the mythological tradition for centuries.

THE DRAMATIC PRESENTATION OF HERAKLES BY EURIPIDES

The Athenian who took his seat in the theater of Dionysos before the performance of Euripides' *Herakles* must have felt keen anticipation and even a touch of excitement. How was Euripides, the least predictable and most challenging of tragic dramatists, going to treat the fate of the Greeks' most important hero? How was he going to wring tragedy from some aspect of the mythical life of a figure who, as the Homeric hymn puts it, 'himself did many wicked things, but also endured many' (*Hymn to Herakles*, 1.6)? Before discussing this question, the chief topic of my essay, let me look briefly at the associations which Herakles' name must have had for our theatergoer, familiar with myth, with Homeric, archaic and classical poetry, and with the Attic stage.

The stories of Herakles, some of which were enshrined in literature by the end of the fifth century B.C., abound in contradictions. The nature of the hero lends itself to such elaboration and expression. Fathered by Zeus, but with mortal mother, Herakles' exploits are shot through with ambiguity as they give witness to the unstable amalgam of human and divine. He is possessed of super-human strength, a legacy from his father, which he uses to a variety of purposes. He slays monsters, opens the way for civilized living, and rewards the favors of friends. The accounts of his remarkable labors change as different cities claim a share in his glory. He has other, less attractive traits. His anger is not to be assuaged, his habits are boorish and gross, and more than once in the epic poems he is described as an unmitigated villain.

At first sight Herakles seems an unlikely tragic hero. His sufferings, occasioned largely by the implacable hatred of Hera, no less than

his successes, belong, we may think, on a plane far removed from the experience and feelings of ordinary humanity. In fact, only few tragedies have Herakles as a central figure and, as we shall see, Euripides has to work hard in his play to anchor the hero, buoyed up by the renown of great deeds, in the world of men.

On the other hand, it is not surprising that the excess which marked Herakles' being was seen as ideal material for treatment in comedy and satyr-drama. Unfortunately, all too little of these dramatic genres has survived, but we can tell from extant plays, fragments, play-titles and the evidence of vase-painting that by the end of the fifth century B.C. Herakles was firmly established in comic and satyric roles.

The traditional stories of Herakles' actions and mode of behavior allowed Old Comedy to highlight several traits of character most suited to its own purposes: brutish manners, a voracious appetite and a prodigious capacity for women. It is clear from the statement in Aristophanes' *Wasps*, 'we have nothing to do with Herakles cheated of his dinner' (1.60), in the middle of a list of traditional comic motifs, that Herakles became one of those figures on which even the most imaginative comedy depends: the predictable buffoon. One of Old Comedy's funniest scenes relies for part of its effect on the pie-in-the-face humor of Herakles' hunger. In Aristophanes' *Birds* 1565 ff. Herakles is part of the legation sent by the gods to Cloudcuckooland; he is prepared to countenance *any* arrangements made between the parties provided that they do not delay lunch.

Burlesque of ancient stories formed the core of satyr-drama, and the exploits of Herakles lent themselves readily to such treatment. His labors, involving as they do super-human struggles against fabulous creatures, cried out for parody and exaggeration. Signs of this are evident even in the scant remains of Euripides' *Syleus*, a play describing Herakles' encounter with the ogre Syleus, who is treated with a violence only barely justified because it is deserved. We get a glimpse of how Herakles' quest for Kerberos might have been treated in satyr-play from a scene in Aristophanes: in *Frogs* 464ff. Aiakos, judge in the underworld, abuses Herakles (alias Dionysos) for stealing Kerberos. The infamous hell-hound is spoken of in terms befitting a favored household pet!

Before leaving this topic and returning to tragedy, I should make some mention of Euripides' treatment of Herakles in the *Alkestis*, a play produced some twenty years earlier than *Herakles*. *Alkestis* is a strange play in which strands of comedy and tragedy intertwine and whose tone is more difficult than usual to determine. The difficulty of the play is likely to be connected with its peculiar generic qualities. *Alkestis* stood forth in a series of productions and so filled the place normally occupied by a satyr-play; it does not contain the basic thematic and formal elements of satyr-drama, but does include some of its characteristics: it is short, has a happy ending reminiscent of folktale, and contains at least one scene which is frankly light-hearted and even comic.

The play is set in Thessaly. Herakles enters on his way to Thrace where he intends to do battle with the man-eating mares of Diomedes, his traditional eighth labor. He has an important role in furthering the plot since in gratitude for Admetos' hospitality he will rescue Alkestis from the grasp of Death and restore her to her bewildered husband. Before this, however, we catch a glimpse of the satyric Herakles discussed above. Euripides makes excellent use of the contrast between the gloom of Admetos' house, lately bereft of its beloved mistress, and the hail-fellow-well-met attitude of the guest Herakles. When he hears that there has been a death in the house, he determines to move on, but persuaded by Admetos' double-talk that the deceased is a stranger, he stays. Hungry as usual, he eats and drinks his fill, and is in no mood to tolerate wet blankets at his private party. When waited on less than enthusiastically by a grieving servant, he abuses the fellow and then tries to cheer him up with some sage advice:

Well, then, get rid of this too-much grief, put flowers on your head and drink with us, fight down these present troubles; later, I know very well that the wine splashing in the bowl will shake you loose from these scowl-faced looks and the tension in your mind. We are only human. Our thoughts should be human too, since, for these solemn people and these people who scowl, the whole parcel of them, if I am any judge, life is not really life but a catastrophe. (11.794ff.)

But Herakles' simple philosophy does not dispel the gloom of the servant who eventually tells him the truth and evokes from him the resolve to rescue Alkestis. By the end of the play the satyric Herakles has receded into the background, and we see instead a character bent not so much on self-gratification as on the role proper to a guest who has enjoyed the inordinate generosity of a friend.

Let us return to the realm of tragedy and examine various presentations of a tragic Herakles. Even though, as we shall see, much of Euripides' picture of Herakles was his own invention, the basic outlines of a human Herakles, a hero capable of suffering and pity, a doer of deeds to be admired and imitated as much as feared had been drawn much earlier. For Pindar, to whom success in athletic contests was a brilliant sign of *arete*, Herakles' strength was a decidedly positive quality. In Pindar's work Herakles' deeds are the model of what strength can achieve. His exploits are stripped of gratuitous violence and the motives for them are purified. Herakles embodies the ideal of strength at the service of others and serves as Pindar's paradigm of true nobility. Pindar's treatment of the hero must have contributed much to the creation of a figure appropriate to tragedy. Herakles continued to share the larger-than-life qualities of an Ajax or an Agamemnon, but he acquired a humanity which allowed for that symphathy on the part of listeners without which tragedy cannot exist.

It is, however, in the poetry of Bacchylides that we see the clearest signs of the nascent tragic Herakles. In his fifth ode, a song in honor of Hiero's victory in the horse race at Olympia in 476 B.C., Bacchylides warns us that it is not the lot of man to be universally happy. This dictum is exemplified by the myth of Herakles' encounter with the shade of Meleager in Hades. On first meeting him, Herakles is terrified and threatens Meleager with his bow. Meleager reassures him, and then explains how he came to die unexpectedly at the height of his powers, destroyed not by some warrior of renown, as Herakles thought, but through the agency of his own mother.

Herakles' reaction to Meleager and his story is remarkable in a number of ways. Herakles is so terrified at the outset that he forgets his bow is useless against the shade of one already dead. Next he asks a question which expresses his constant dread of Hera: 'Who killed you? Soon will deep-girdled Hera send him against my person' (1.89). After hearing Meleager's story, he bursts into tears and utters a traditional dictum which comes as a surprise from the greatest and most successful of heroes: 'Best it is for mortals not to be born and not to look on the light of the sun' (1.160). The myth closes with Herakles' inquiring after marriage prospects among Meleager's sisters; he is told of Deianeira, who will indeed become his wife and will be, like Meleager's mother, responsible for his death.

Bacchylides' characterization of Herakles is done within a moment, yet the deft touches emphasized above are sufficient to invest the hero with the humanity, even the frailty, which fitted him for development as a tragic figure. In a strange world Herakles can feel terror, can be foolish. No matter where he is, he seems to be constantly in the shadow of Hera's jealous designs on his life. The great son of Amphitryon can feel to the point of tears the fragility of man's lot, but determines to find some solace in action, action which we know will destroy him no less unexpectedly than Meleager. Here we find a most poignant touch in Bacchylides' picture of Herakles. With great naturalness the man of strength turns to *praxis*, activity, as the only course open to mortals in a world fraught with uncertainty. The ultimate sadness is that he cannot know that this, too, is futile.

Such, then, were the preconceptions about the life and character of Herakles which the Athenian theater-goer brought to the performance of Euripides' play, produced, it is likely, a year or two before 415 B.C. He also had in mind Sophokles' dramatization of the hero's final moments in the *Trachiniai*, a play produced probably two or three decades earlier. Sophokles had dwelt with terrifying effect on Herakles' proneness to violence, on his more than human anger, and on the extreme physical pain he endured before his death. The suffering of Euripides' hero will be different; equally intense, it is occasioned by the tearing apart not of his body, but of the network of emotional ties which supports him.

The very beginning of the play indicates Euripides' penchant for modifying existing tradition. The scene is Thebes: sitting as suppliants at an altar are Herakles' father, wife and three sons. They are threatened by Lykos, usurper of Thebes' throne, who imagines, incorrectly in this play, that Herakles is dead and who wants to secure his position from any threats the children may pose after they reach manhood. The idea that Herakles is away, completing in Hades his final labor while his sons are still alive is Euripides' invention. The dominant tradition, it seems, had Herakles perform his labors *after* the murder of his sons.

Despite these striking innovations, the first part of the play must have created little excitement and aroused few deep emotions. The conflict between Lykos and his victims involves much that is predictable; there is a good deal of frigid argument and an unusual amount of repetition. The unexpected return of Herakles may have brought the audience to the edge of their seats for a moment, but it is unlikely that anyone shared with conviction the despairing belief of the family that the hero was gone for ever. That Herakles should return, dispatch the villain and regain his rightful position of authority is scarcely an unusual plot. Even the characters of the opening scenes are far from engaging. The villain Lykos is drawn too simply to be interesting, and neither Megara nor Amphitryon touch us deeply with their over-indulgence in rhetoric and their concerns with artificial-sounding questions. To sum up: the first part of the play generates complacency rather than tragic bewilderment. If Euripides seems to have let us down, the reason is that we have seen only half the play and that his attention has been not so much on the characters on stage as on the absent Herakles. The hero is on stage for only 100 of the play's first 800 lines, yet he is kept, even before he first appears, continuously before our minds. The dramatist wants to make certain that we are clear about *his* conception of this multifaceted figure.

After some doubts about the place of justice and Zeus' care for his offspring, the hero's return puts all to rights and the audience can say with the chorus:

Disaster is reversed!
The tyrant's life turns back to Hades!
Justice flows back! O fate of the gods,
returning!
Your time has come. You go now where the price
for outrage on your betters must be paid.
  Joy once more! Overboard with grief!
  The king has come again!
  He has come, of whom I had no hope,
  my country's king, come back again!   (11.734 ff.)

Euripides is careful first of all to purify the motives for Herakles' deeds. In the tradition of Pindar, he is at pains to show that the labors were performed not as a consequence of some praeter-natural love of violence, but to benefit his father and under the compulsion of Hera or fate. The labors themselves are presented in the beautiful first stasimon (11.348 ff.) as deeds performed in the interests of mankind, whose world is made more habitable by Herakles' toils. There is no sense of indulgence in violence for its own sake, no aggrandizement of self in a context divorced from the good of one's family and friends. This point is brought out in the strangely prolonged debate between Lykos and Amphitryon on the reality of Herakles' glorious deeds (11.140 ff.). Amphitryon's repudiation of the tyrant's sneers lends the authority of anticipation to the chorus' song and at the same time lays stress on the connection between Herakles' actions and the stature and fate of his family.

The emphasis on the positive quality of the labors engages strongly the audience's sympathy for the hero on his return. We share his outrage at the fact that his family, despite his benefactions, have been harassed with impunity. At the same time we share the confidence of Amphitryon and the others that the man whose *arete* had been sung in the ode will not allow Lykos his head for very much longer. The words threatening violence in 11.566 ff. have occasioned misgivings in the minds of some critics who believe that Euripides is giving us here a glimpse of a Herakles who is already unbalanced in his attachment to deeds of blood. I should say, with the chorus, that the outburst is justified. Granted the vengeance is to be on an epic scale; but can we expect less from the tamer of monsters when he acts in defense of his loved ones?

But more important to Euripides, I believe, than the purification of Herakles' motives is the domestication of his person. The dramatist is lavish in the detail he devotes, both before and after the hero's appearance, to Herakles' relationship with his children, his concern for them and the affection they have for their father. Very early in the play a speech of Megara presents a vignette, at once charming and pathetic, of the children's behavior at home during his absence:

> First one, then another, bursts in tears,
> and asks: "Mother, where has Father gone?
> What is he doing? When will he come back?"
> Then, too small to understand, they ask again
> for "Father." I put them off with stories;
> but when the hinges creak, they all leap up
> to run and throw themselves at their father's feet.
> (11.73 ff.)

Later on Megara gives us a glimpse of them at play. Again, their father is very much at the center of things and Euripides skillfully converts the signs of Herakles' superhuman valor into objects of fun, which, instead of taking him out of his children's world, bring them into his:

> To *you* your father would have left all Argos:
> in Eurystheus' halls you would have ruled
> and held the sway over rich Pelasgia.
> It was upon your head he sometimes threw
> the skin of tawny lion that he wore.
> *You*, made king of chariot-loving Thebes,
> would have inherited your mother's lands,
> because you teased them from your father once.
> Sometimes in play, he put in your right hand
> that carven club he kept for self-defense.
> (11.462 ff.)

The impression gained after Herakles' return is no different. The children run to greet him, cling to his garments and refuse to let him go. In the end he goes inside with them, treating them with the same playful indulgence hinted at in the previous passage:

> Look:
> They will not let me go, but clutch my clothes
> more tightly. How close you came to death!
> Here, I'll take your hands and lead you in my wake,
> like a ship that tows its little boats behind,
> for I accept this care and service
> of my sons. Here all mankind is equal:
> rich and poor alike, they love their children.
> (11.629 ff.)

These little scenes are created not merely for the sake of sentimental pathos. They are used to put Herakles in his place. The renowned deeds of the hero, celebrated by the chorus in the first stasimon, had the world for their theater. But Euripides wants to anchor the hero more firmly at home and to show us the depth and tragic significance of actions performed there. The picture of Herakles bringing peace and security to his family is vital to the development of the play. The images created by the passages quoted above are meant to persist in our minds until they recur, grotesquely transformed, in the play's second part.

For now we enjoy a state of apparent equilibrium. Another monster has been dealt with, and the gods have shown their concern for just and unjust alike. The play could well end here as a complete, if not very satisfying, melodrama. But the sense of resolution of doubts and restoration of order has been created only as a foil to the sequel: the annihilation of Herakles' world, his grief and despair, and his eventual rehabilitation through the help of a friend.

No sooner has the chorus celebrated the death of Lykos than Hera strikes. Suddenly there appear above the stage-building Iris, messenger of the gods and Hera's agent, and Lyssa, the personification of madness. Lyssa is goaded into attacking the mind of Herakles and driving him to kill his wife and children in a fit of madness.

The change which comes over the hero and his subsequent actions are described in one of tragedy's most chilling speeches. The account of Herakles' seizure, the bewildered questions of father and servants, the pleas of children and wife spare our feelings very little. The death of each child is described in all too much macabre detail, and we share to the full Amphitryon's relief at the appearance of Athena, who strikes Herakles senseless just before he adds parricide to his crimes.

The horror we feel before Herakles' murders has a special quality for two reasons. First, we are made acutely aware of the inversion of reality which they represent: the saviour has become slayer; the strength once used on behalf of his family has now destroyed them; the home which he greeted so fondly after his return and to which he restored his children is the site of the hero's demented rampage. Even the detail of earlier scenes contributes to this effect. The club earlier given to the boy as a plaything is seen in its true light as a murder weapon.

The second reason for our shock at Herakles' crimes is that they are inexplicable in human terms. Filled with pity and fear, we ask the question 'why' just as Lyssa herself asks it. She affirms in her dialogue with Iris that Herakles is unworthy of punishment: his actions both in the distant and immediate past are beyond reproach; he has acted in concert with the gods and for the good of men. We might say simply that Hera destroys Herakles for reasons which do not go beyond her traditional enmity towards him. But what of Iris' statement in 1.841: 'the gods will be nowhere, and mortal affairs will be great, if he does not pay the penalty'? This implies that Herakles has done some wrong—a wrong which it is difficult to identify. Perhaps Euripides is telling us that divine notions of what deserves punishment are different from ours. For Hera the crime of Herakles is, first, that he exists as the son of her faithless husband, and, second, that his extraordinary success draws attention to his divine origins. Only when he is brought low, when he is stripped of his supernatural qualities and is seen as fully human, indeed less than human, will she be able to tolerate his existence.

The report of Herakles' murders is followed by choral lament and then, by means of stage machinery, the inside of the house is 'wheeled out' so that the scene of the slaughter becomes visible. We find Herakles asleep amidst the corpses of his loved ones; beside them stands the aged, grieving father who begs the chorus not to rouse his son. It is hard to imagine a scene more touching than this. The great hero, personification of strength and valour, lies senseless and in need of such protection as his father can give. But worse is to come, for Herakles has yet to learn what he had done, and this awareness comes only after a painful discussion with Amphitryon. His immediate reaction is to end his own life and take vengeance once again, in a perverted sense, on anyone who harms his family.

Euripides could have ended the play with this decision and left us with Herakles for whom life on the terms dictated by Hera was not worth living. Such a figure would have shared the fate of Sophokles' Ajax and been no less impressive. But Euripides has a different ending in mind, one in which Herakles continues to live not as a demi-god, but as a mere mortal.

In the final section of the play Euripides introduces a further modification of the traditional story in the person of Theseus who, having heard of trouble in Thebes, arrives unexpectedly from Athens. He is too late to help with the removal of Lycus, but finds instead a situation far more painful than civil disturbance and a Herakles bent on self-destruction. Herakles, so often the support for others, must now himself rely on his friend to find reasons for continuing to live. Theseus provides a place to live and the support of a friendship undeterred by considerations of blood-guilt and pollution. But, most importantly, he encourages Herakles to come to terms with his humanity, crushed though it be, and to continue to live, if not as the glorious son of Zeus, then as the son of Amphitryon whose fame is no accident of birth. As Theseus reminds him, Herakles is not a man 'such as one might meet by chance.' The renown he has enjoyed can continue to be his, but on different grounds. It will not rest on his divine pedigree, but on his human *arete* which allows him, with the support of friends, to rise above Hera's attacks.

The play's closing moments are a wonderful affirmation of the strength of humanity in the face of an unpredictable and hostile universe. Herakles leaves for Athens determined to live, but weak and clinging to his friend for support.

We are reminded very deliberately of an earlier scene when Herakles took his frightened children into the house. Euripides uses the recurrent image not simply to underline the catastrophic change in Herakles' fortunes, but to show us what can and must remain constant and immutable if life is to go on: not wealth nor strength, but love and friends.

Bibliographic Note:

Translations are from *Euripides*, Richmond Lattimore, editor, "Alcestis," translated by Richmond Lattimore, and "Heracles," volume 2, translated by W. Arrowsmith. Chicago, University of Chicago Press, copyright 1955.

HERAKLES IN PINDAR

Of all the ancient poets who celebrated Herakles, Pindar alone has the distinction of having been his fellow-citizen. Both were born in Thebes, a fact that Pindar stitches again and again into the weft of his verse: he rarely mentions himself except as a "dweller by the waters of Dirke," and often when he speaks of Herakles it is to stress his Theban origins. Like Herakles, moreover, his calling led him to traverse the lengths of the Mediterranean world, fulfilling commissions from patrons as far east as Rhodes, as far west as Sicily, as far south as Cyrene. In so doing he composed a poetry of deliberately pan-Hellenic scope which at the same time never failed to pay special honor to the heroes associated with each city it touched on. That the greatest of all heroes was associated with his own city seems to have provided a special theme for Pindar's meditation.

Taking the forty-five complete epinicians (victory odes for athletes) and the fragments from the other genres in which Pindar composed, it is easy, by making a preliminary catalogue of the episodes from Herakles' life that appear there, to see which are repeated most often and which loom largest. His siring by Zeus and birth to Alkmene is repeatedly mentioned (*Pythian 9, Nemean 1, Nemean 10, Isthmian 7*), usually in the course of cataloguing glories of the past. His prodigious first feat, strangling the snakes that attacked him in his cradle, is recounted in a full-dress narrative that occupies most of *Nemean 1* (cf. Cat. No. 37). Of the canonical labors most are mentioned only once in passing: the Nemean lion (*Isthmian 6*; cf. Cat. No. 3,14,59), the golden hind (*Olympian 3*), the Augeian stables (*Olympian 10*; cf. Cat. No. 38), the horses of Diomedes (Fr. 169, Snell edition) and the battle with Kyknos on the same trip (*Olympian 10*; cf.

Cat. No. 1,17), the cattle of Geryon (Fr. 169, *Isthmian 1*; cf. Cat. No. 7) and the wrestling with Antaios that occurred *en route* (*Isthmian 4*), the expedition against the Amazons (Fr. 172). On the same voyage as this last labor, however, Herakles and the heroes he assembled round him sacked Troy in punishment for the deceit of Laomedon, and the frequency with which Pindar praises the sack (*Olympian 8, Nemean 4, Isthmian 5, Isthmian 6*, Fr. 172) makes it clear that he deemed the first Trojan war no less worthy of song than the later one whose episodes he always mentions in praise of Achilles. Likewise, on a side trip from his encounter with Antaios in Africa Herakles went to the straits of Gibraltar and set up his famous pillars, proclaiming that there was no further passage westward (*Olympian 3, Nemean 3, Nemean 4, Isthmian 4*), a civilizing act which for Pindar seems to have had more symbolic resonance than any of the monster-slayings. Most solemnly recounted of all, and understandably so in the victory-odes, is the pious son's founding of the Olympic games in honor of his father Zeus (*Olympian 3, Olympian 10*). Beyond that supreme achievement there was only the hero's apotheosis, in which he married immortal Youth and took up residence forever in the golden halls of Olympos (*Nemean 1, Nemean 10, Isthmian 4*). For Pindar this assumption is always an effortlessly accomplished fact; there is no trace of the final consuming pyre on Mt. Oita which in Sophokles' *Trachiniae* becomes the image of "tragedy wrought to its uttermost."

However, if we were content with a catalogue of these episodes laid out in the chronological order of Herakles' life, we would violate the essential procedure of Pindar's poems. For his is an art of selection, juxtaposition, and significant rearrangement of chronological sequence, and the placement of a mythical allusion in the evolution of an ode is as crucial as the relative amount of space it occupies. Just as in a museum exhibition the curator must reconstitute for each object the world of its commissioning, its purposes, and the physical location for which it was intended, so, if we cite Pindar's verses on various myths, everything depends on giving the verses body by locating them in the ode's larger strategies. Only through these strategies does one approach the real depth of Pindar's thought; and Herakles was a theme by which his depths were stirred.

This was true not only because the two men were fellow Thebans but because Herakles was the only hero to become a god. When Pindar calls him *heros theos*, "the hero-god" (*Nemean 3* 1.22; the phrase is set at the beginning of a triad, a musical and choreographic unit in the ode's performance, and would have stood out in bold relief), he does so to stress the awesome uniqueness of this conflation of categories everywhere else kept rigidly separate. The world of the victory-ode is normally structured by the three-fold distinction among gods, heroes and men, and meaning is secured by defining their modes of mutual relation. As an athletic victor, the living man, whom it was the ode's primary purpose to praise, suggested the possibility that, however briefly, mortal lives can be irradiated by the favor of the immortals. Athletes won in games which were rites in a god's honor at a sacred precinct, and their victory had always to be attributed to a mysterious conjunction of their own merits and the god's choice. The beginning and end of the ode would be taken up with this praise, and the mythical mid-section would normally consist of material from heroic legend whose analogy to the athlete's case was that, in those great ages of the past, too, divine favor had touched certain men and driven them to stand out from the crowd. The *charis* between man and god, that joy of mutuality between a giver and a receiver, may have been only momentary, as in the case of the athlete, or may have been sustained for a whole lifetime, as in the case of some of the heroes. But it remained grounded in the pathos of a giver who would never die and a receiver who was destined to do so. In becoming an Olympian, Herakles transcended this pathos and became the only person in poetic song who could stand on either side of the mutual joy between gods and men, sometimes recipient of favor, sometimes bestower of it.

In only one ode, *Isthmian 4*, is the complete cycle of Herakles' fate set out in anything like chronological order. Composed for a fellow Theban who had triumphed at local games in Herakles' honor, as well as at the Isthmos, the ode first introduces the hero's name in the course of praising the larger achievements of the athlete's whole clan:

> By their supreme feats of courage
> they set out from home
>   and reached the Pillars of Herakles:
>
> they have no need of further glory.
>
> (I.4.11-13)

(All translations are by Frank J. Nisetich, *Pindar's Victory Songs*, The Johns Hopkins University Press, copyright 1980.)

Here, as in all the other passages in which they are mentioned, the Pillars of Herakles are transformed by Pindar from geographical limits on men's wanderings into symbolic limits on their possibilities of happiness. They thus present us with the paradox that the man who defined those horizontal limits was the man who, in his vertical ascent to Olympos, went beyond the limits of happiness for which they came to stand. As it comes to the full story of Herakles in its final stretch, the ode seems to wish to let the mystery speak for itself:

> A man, small in build
> but adamant in spirit,
> once went from Kadmeian Thebes to wheat-bearing
>   Libya
> to the house of Antaios,
>   to wrestle him
> and put an end to his roofing Poseidon's temple
> with the skulls of strangers—
>   it was he,
>
> Alkmena's son, who reached Olympos
>   when he had explored the earth
>   from end to end,
>   and even the chasmed hollow of the gray ocean bed,
> and had smoothed the way
>   for sailing ships.
> Now he abides with aegis-bearing Zeus,
>   embracing perfect happiness,
>   and he has won glory
>   in the friendship of the immortals,
> with Hebe for his bride,
>   lord of a golden house and son-in-law of Hera.
>
> For him we citizens of Thebes
>   spread the feast
>   outside the Elektran Gate
>   and lay fresh garlands on his altars,
> heaping high the flame of sacrifice
>   to the eight who died—
> wielders of bronze swords:
>   Megara, Kreon's daughter, bore them to him,
>   his sons, for whom, at dusk,

the rising blaze burns, unceasing
through the night,
     grazing heaven with its fragrant smoke.
And all through the following day
there is the culmination, the yearly games,
the work of might.

               (I.4.70-86)

The cyclical repetition of athletic games at
Thebes in Herakles' honor seems, in Pindar's
ordering of elements here, to be an essential
part of his account if the hero's fate is to be
understood. Linear chronology breaks down
when a mortal ceases to have a lifeline with an
end as well as a beginning, and the cyclical time
of civic ritual becomes our only handle on the
heavenly time into which he has been transumed.

In all the other odes in which Herakles is the
principal figure chosen from heroic legend,
Pindar seems to avoid assuming the full burden
of the mystery, preferring to focus instead on
an episode during his earthly lifetime in which,
while himself still the recipient of divine favor,
he also already appears as a benefactor to his
fellow men. *Isthmian 6* is a perfectly wrought
specimen of this focusing technique, setting at
its center the image of the hero wrapped in the
lion skin so prevalent in visual representations:

       But when he came to summon
Telamon upon that journey,
     he found him at a feast.
         And Telamon invited him,
         the son of Amphitryon,
    mighty with his spear, standing
in his lion's pelt,
         to lead the way
with nektar-sweet libations
    and offered him
      the wine-bowl
        glittering with gold.
         And Herakles, raising
invincible hands toward the sky,
           uttered this prayer:
"If ever, O father Zeus,
    with willing heart you heard my entreaties,

now I beseech you, now, in supplication:
bring to birth from Eriboia a mighty son,
destined to be my guest-friend,
         for Telamon here, a son
unbreakable in body, even as the hide
that winds about me now, the skin of the lion
I killed at Nemea, foremost
of all my exploits;
         and may he have
a lion's courage."
When he had spoken thus,
the god sent down a great eagle, prince of birds,
and a sweet joy thrilled within him . . .

             (I.6.35-50)

The eagle (*aietos*) Zeus sends stirs Herakles to
prophesy to Telamon that he will have a mighty
son named Aias, and the swiftness with which
Zeus sends a sign in response to his prayer
brings Herakles joy. Here too the word *charis*,
denoting the joy stirred in a mortal by a sign of
favor from a god, is carefully positioned as the
last word of the central triad of the ode, thus
giving a choreographic frame to the verbal
tableau.

Herakles' benefaction here is a simple kind-
ness to a friend, and if Pindar has set the episode in high relief it is because his main concern
is to establish the epinician's prime point of
analogy: the hero, like the athlete, is seen mo-
mentarily bathed in the radiance of an Olympian's attention. In *Olympian 3*, by contrast, the
emphasis shifts to his role as an intermediary
between mortal athletes and the full glare of
divinity that shines upon them. There the story
is told of his bringing olive trees to shade the
newly cleared site of the Olympic contests:

     Already had the Moon at midmonth
        made the whole eye of evening
shine upon him from her golden car,

and he had set up the sacred judgement of the contests
      and the five-year festival
         upon the hallowed banks of Alpheos—
          but the ground in the valley
of Kronian Pelops had not yet put forth
its radiant forest, and naked of that
        the garden seemed to him
          defenseless against the sun's sharp rays . . .

             (O.3.19-24)

The moment he finishes his planting, the ode
shifts, as in *Isthmian 4*, from narrative of the
heroic past to invocation of the cyclical time of
the ritual present:

       And now to this feast he comes in good cheer
with the twin sons of slim-waisted Leda.

For to them he entrusted the care
     of the contests of men
       and the swift cars of the racing
         as he went on his way to Olympos.

             (O.3.34-38)

Thus in the independent pattern created by
this particular ode's selection and arrangement
of episodes, the shielding of men from heavenly radiance becomes the last act of Herakles
before he himself enters that radiance, there
to abide forever, except when he is imagined
as a guest returning to the earthly festival he
founded in his Olympian father's honor. His
benefaction to men consists in acknowledg-

ing their inability to sustain the uninterrupted glory he alone among them is about to take on.

The foundation of the Olympic games is also the subject of the grandest of Pindar's compositions in which Herakles is the theme of the mythical centerpiece, *Olympian 10*. In some odes his violence comes to the fore, as manslaughterer and monster-slayer, and in others he is the civilizer who sets up boundaries and clears sacred spaces. But in *Olympian 10* the violence is given its full due in the second of the ode's five triads, narrating his fierce vengeance on Augeias for not paying him his wages. This creates all the more foil for the solemnity of the third and fourth triads, in which the Olympic precinct is cleared and the first games are celebrated. As the choreographic design reaches its precise center in the third triad, Pindar names the divine presences standing at Herakles' side at that foundational moment—the Fates (Moïrai) and Time itself:

> Then Zeus' warlike son drew his entire host
> together in Pisa,
>   all the booty skimmed
>   from the heap of battle.
>   He marked out a precinct sacred
> to his father,
>   fenced the Altis apart in the clear
> and made the plain around
>   a place for feasting,
>   honoring the ford of Alpheos
>
> and the twelve lordly gods:
>   he called it Kronos' Hill,
>   for in former times,
>   when Oinomaos ruled,
>   it had lain beneath deep drifts
> of snow, without a name.
>   Now, at its first birth rites,
> the Moirai stood by, and next to them
>   the one
>   who alone proves Truth true,
>
> Time,
>   and Time moving onward
> has made it manifest:
> how Herakles set war's first fruits
> aside for sacrifice and ordained
> the five-year festival
> with the first Olympiad and its triumphs.
>
> (O.10.43-59)

After the roll of the first set of Olympic victors is called, Pindar makes his familiar return to his own present in its cyclical repetition of the past:

> And then the radiance
> of the moon's beautiful eye made evening shine.

All the precinct rang with music, sung at the feast
in the mode of praise.
            Following those beginnings,
let us even now
sing the song named for victory . . .

(O.10.73-79)

But clearly it has been no ordinary epiphany of divine favor that accompanied Herakles' act of foundation. Not Zeus or any other Olympian, but these more abstract beings, the Fates and Time, stood by his side when he performed what for Pindar is the consummation of his life's task, the supremely pious and civilizing act to which all the slaughters were merely a necessary prelude. Herakles is the one mortal who was himself fated to overcome the Time to which all others are subject. In that curious fusion of the abstract and the sensuous of which archaic thought was still capable, Pindar has created a tableau out of these hypostatizations at the hero's side—Time like a chorus leader, the Fates his chorus—and set it at the center of his own choreographic design.

It is only when we move with ease among these hypostatized beings that we can begin to hear some of the meanings in perhaps the gravest of Pindar's meditations, *Nemean 7*, which begins and ends by naming the bride who symbolized Herakles' eternal happiness, Hebe. Hebe means simply youth or adolescence in Greek, the time when young women were given in marriage and young men began to test themselves in the games. Zeus himself was Hebe's father, and in giving her in marriage to Herakles on his translation to Olympos he gave the surest pledge of the mortal hero's transformation into an immortal. *Nemean 7*, for reasons presumably having to do with the family of its subject, Sogenes or "Savior of the Stock," is preoccupied with the darkness that besets the course of a mortal's span, both the obscurity and distortion of his fame that may come after his death and the many dangers that can keep him from coming to a good old age in calm contemplation of his posterity. It is accordingly no accident that the beginning of the ode is a prayer to Eleithyia, goddess of childbirth, in conjunction with the Moirai and Hebe, and that its conclusion is a prayer to Herakles himself in which Hebe is again drawn in, now simply as the word for "youth" as opposed to "old age." The opening prayer is reminiscent of a sculptural composition in the way it groups the goddesses next to each other:

Eleithyia, enthroned beside the profound Moirai,
    daughter of Hera in her great strength,
hear me, deliverer of children:
                without you
  we can have no vision
    of day or dark night,
      no share in the blessings
of Hebe, your sister, with the shining limbs.

                        (N.7.1-4)

The concluding prayer, addressed to Herakles as "slayer of giants" and "blessed one," likewise invokes him as a cult presence in his shrine on Aegina, next to which Sogenes and his father lived, and the intimate details of topography seem appropriate to the neighborly solicitude the hero-god is being asked to show:

              If one man
has any knowledge of another,
    he would say
      a loving-minded neighbor
is a joy to value over all.
And if a god as well
            endorse that precept,
Sogenes would pray
  to go on dwelling
    through your grace,
      O slayer of giants,
             in good fortune
and devotion to his father,
  in the richly built
sacred avenue
        where his ancestors have dwelt—

for he has his house between your holy grounds,
  like the yoke in a four-horse chariot,
to right and left of him
           as he approaches.
  O blessed one,
    it is fitting
      that you should sway
the heart of Hera's consort
and his bright-eyed daughter's will.
    Often you are able
to give men strength
  in intractable disasters.
    So may you join
      to his youth
        and shining old age
a life of enduring vigor, weaving it through
  happily to its end,
and may
    his children's children enjoy forever

the honor of this moment
        and more in after time.

                  (N. 10.86-101)

We are not told what "intractable disasters" might have darkened the history of this clan, but the information is not necessary to establish the poignance of the prayer to the supreme hero to help us find our own reserves of strength. One catches here better than anywhere else in Pindar the intimacy of the tone with which the Theban poet prays to his fellow, once a man and now a god. It is precisely because Herakles once experienced himself as a mortal that he can now be asked, in a way no other god could be, to lend strength as our inescapable mortality presses on us. Again and again associated with Time, with Fate, with Youth, he gives human meaning to these abstractions precisely because he has lived through them and comes out on the other side. His favor, when he bestows it, has a pathos no born Olympian can know.

Pindar's personal bond with the supreme hero, then, need not be seen as merely rooted in chauvinism. The way of thinking that led the citizens of the various Greek city-states to pray to the heroes whose shrines they grew up among was itself an acknowledgement of our mortal limitations, what is local and partial being our proper avenue of access to what is universal and complete. If the Greek world agreed in believing that one hero, and one only, had passed beyond all partial limitation to the status of an Olympian god, all the more reason not to set him beyond our reach by forgetting the nurture he once received from a particular mother and a particular place. If he now dwelled in heaven, his mother Alkmene was still a presence in Thebes; in the opening of *Pythian 11* we catch a glimpse of her in a consort of numinous ladies making their way to the Ismenion, a temple just outside the city, "where even now/ the god bids his band of heroines,/dwellers in this country/to gather in procession/at height of evening . . ." (P.1.1-10). Pindar proudly expected that any Greek would readily give the Theban hero praise. He also kept a special faith with Herakles befitting the fact that they had known the same nurture and drunk of the same streams. As god who presides over the successful completion of a mortal lifespan, Herakles was to remain on the poet's lips as long as the poet could sing:

       . . . dumb is the man who does not crown
  Herakles with praise, or revere
    the springs of Dirka
that nursed both him and Iphikles.
To them will I sing whenever good befalls me
  and so fulfill my vow.

                  (P.9.87-90)

HERCULES AS HERO
FOR SENECA

Today's rather diffuse concept of the 'hero' serves mainly the purposes of news reporters and teen-agers. He is a role-model who has done something extraordinary in war or fire-rescuing, in space-travel or in pop-music—extraordinary but not forever beyond the reach of his acolytes. The hero of classical legend was of another breed. Usually with one divine parent, he was a performer of salutary and spectacular deeds that demanded his superhuman courage, strength, and skill; and yet —by token of his mixed parentage—he served as an available intermediary between mankind and the gods. Of such heroes, Hercules, who had close analogues in most of the other cultures/religions of the Middle East, probably had the greatest range of talents and facets: strong-man par excellence, bully, rescuer of women and children, clown, lover, tamer of untamable animals and forces of nature. These varied aspects of Hercules are widely reflected in the many, often complex or ambiguous, representations of his life and deeds in classical art and literature.

To understand the multiple facets of Hercules we must look at the nature of 'myth.' Every user of a myth, whether in drama, statue, opera, or political cartoon, is willy-nilly a re-molder or recreator of the myth—fitting it to his times, circumstances, or needs. Not in the constancy of a tradition, but in this individuated plasticity lies the vitality of myth and legend. This protean quality is built into the history of most of the major figures of Greek and Roman myth.

'Greece' and 'Rome' were, like many of the nations new in the present century, synthetic agglomerations: ill-assorted regions and peoples jammed together by conquest, by fiat, or by necessity, in the hope that by the blood of their brows they would stick together. Like many of today's new nations, 'Greece' and 'Rome' each had a long and troubled history trying to achieve peace or unity within their borders. In these ancient nations a conscious effort to bring about religious unity was one of the major peace-making devices. Thus ten or twenty local divinities having some conceivable relation to Apollo were brought together under the rubric of 'Apollo'—often with some restrictive epithet (Phoebus, Sminthian, or the like), even though the resultant divinity might wind up being a teratological combination of Healer and Destroyer, Sun-God, Mouse-God, Frog-God.

But this complexity within the god, goddess, or hero was only one of the great problems facing the Greek tragic poets who utilized the legends. Even greater was the distance in time, beliefs, and customs between the mythopoeic era and the generations in which the plays were written. These problems might be thus envisioned: 'How are we, writing in and for the enlightened generation of Pericles, in a theater which is a temple of Dionysus, himself anciently imported to our land from the distant East—how are we to deal with these legends from the sacred past of our religion, whose simplistic explanation of God-manipulated behavior we can no longer accept, and yet cannot reject?' And so Aeschylus, writing of the death of Agamemnon, has Clytemnestra kill him for six good wifely reasons, believable by any wife even today; Homer, centuries earlier, had had the killing done by Aegisthus, lover of Clytemnestra and inheritor of a family blood-curse in which Clytemnestra had no part.

Seneca felt no obligation to bow to history or to religion. Roman drama had long since departed from the temple of Dionysus, and the

Romans had only a weak tradition of lineal descent from the ancient gods and heroes. Rather, Seneca's plays are informed by the central force of his own life: a combination of Roman *gravitas*, of a deep awareness of the gruesome and awesome extremes possible to men and women of great power, and of a teacher's/philosopher's impulse to instruct by stark example. These qualities can be seen in comparing Seneca's plays with their Greek analogues. Seneca's Hercules (especially in the *Hercules Furens*) is formally more tidy, more subtle in depiction of character, and more psychologically convincing to us than Euripides' Herakles.This may at first sound surprising, but remember that the Greek plays, though unquestionably greater, are also more remote from us—not merely in time, but, more importantly, in their impact on European drama. The drama of the ancient Greeks, for all its greatness, has had little influence on the art or structure of later drama.

Yet every Roman writer lived with the specter of Greek predecessors peering over both shoulders. Both Plautus and Terence wrote their comedies as acknowledged paraphrases or derivatives of Greek models (Terence was called, by Julius Caesar, *dimidiate Menander*—half a Menander); Virgil for a long time was seen as a pallid and subservient imitator of Homer; Seneca himself faced his readers as a lurid yet forceless Euripides. But perceptions change. We need not deny the greatness, even the superiority, of the Greeks. But an imitator may, even unconsciously, do something far beyond imitation. Plautus, Terence, and Virgil stand on their own feet today: the social circumstances and the individual aims of these Roman 'imitators' were so radically different from their Greek 'originals' that the resultant plays and epic poems could not help having new foundations, new purposes.

The character of Hercules, especially in the *Furens*, provides a good instance of Seneca's dramatic aims. In this work the hero, of semidivine parentage, is a man endowed by fortune not only with many extraordinary strengths but also with great tenderness for his wife and children. His deeds of strength, daring, and benevolence were part of the myth and folklore of a great portion of the Mediterranean world. That Jupiter was his father (and was thus the source of his powers) and that Juno bore him eternal hatred (and thus became the external motivating force for many of his deeds) were essential components of his story. Seneca's interest was not in the Twelve Great Tasks;

these and other feats of strength and daring stand as the known background and potentiality of the hero. What Seneca shows is the spoiled part of the picture. Whether brought about by Juno's malevolence (as she promises in the prologue to the *Furens*), by his own arrogance, or by the pure nastiness of events, Hercules' glorious, even messianic, career ends in madness, filicide, and in the *Oeta*, in a particularly painful death.

The two plays about Hercules constitute a curiously interwoven pair, as though, in a plan to construct the ideal Stoic hero/god, Seneca was as careful to avoid repetition as to achieve completeness. In the first play, *Hercules Furens* (Mad, or Raging), Hercules returns to Thebes from the Underworld, where he had had the mission of capturing Cerberus. In Thebes he finds that King Creon has been killed by Lycus, who has seized the royal power, and now wishes to marry Hercules' wife Megara, of the royal family of Thebes, to consolidate his descendants' hold on the throne. Hercules kills Lycus, but, driven mad by Juno, goes on to kill Megara and their children. Sane again, he wishes to kill himself, but his friend Theseus, King of Athens, who had accompanied him to the Underworld, persuades him to take refuge in Athens. Seneca's play is based on Euripides' *Herakles* but is notably more tightly knit in plot and more consistent in character.

Seneca's *Hercules on Oeta* is derived from Sophocles' *Trachiniae*, with some details borrowed from Ovid's *Metamorphoses* and *Heroides*. The story of the play turns on the revenge of the centaur Nessus, who had received his death-blow in an attempt to kidnap Deianeira, wife of Hercules. As he lay dying, Nessus told Deianeira that a robe dipped in his blood would bring Hercules back to her if he should stray to another woman. Sophocles' play had shown Deianeira as a devoted wife, whose attempt to regain her husband ended in catastrophe; she sent the robe to Hercules when he seemed to be pursuing Iole, but the robe, poisoned by the alien blood of Nessus, inflicted an agonizing death on Hercules. Seneca transformed the story by placing the focus on Hercules in both halves of the play: the play opens by showing him as a noble conqueror. When Deianeira appears, her jealousy and violence make her somewhat less symphathetic than Sophocles's Deianeira had been. Hercules suffers, dies, and appears —deified—after his death, the idealized representation of the Stoic hero, victorious even over death.

One mark of Seneca as dramatist (perhaps

the strongest internal evidence that he wrote for stage presentation) is the *kind* of attention he pays to minor characters, rounding them out, justifying them as human beings. Thus Juno speaks the prologue of the *Hercules Furens*, with little more dramatic point than to tell us of her hatred for Hercules and of her intent to destroy him. Yet while she is doing this she is fair-minded enough to give an almost admiring account of his great deeds (I quote from *Seneca, in Ten Volumes*, Vols. 8 and 9. Translated by Frank Justus Miller, Loeb Classical Library, copyright 1979):

... Whatever fearsome creature the hostile earth produces, whatever the sea or air has borne, terrific, dreadful, noxious, savage, wild, has been broken and subdued ... Where the Sun, as he brings back, and where, as he dismisses day, colours both Ethiop races with neighboring torch, his unconquered valour is adored, and in all the world he is storied as a god. Now I have no monsters left, and 'tis less labour for Hercules to fulfill my orders than for me to order; with joy he welcomes my commands.
(30-42)

An even better instance of Seneca's even-handedness comes in the opening lines of the play (Juno speaks):

The sister of the Thunderer (for this name only is left to me), I have abandoned Jove, always another's lover, widowed, have left the spaces of high heaven and, banished from the sky, have given up my place to harlots; I must dwell on earth, for harlots hold the sky.

(We must remember how many of the constellations were named from one or another of Jove's love-affairs.) Heaven, once her home and realm, became so unbearable, it was abandoned; Hercules, as the product of one of the most notorious of Jove's affairs, has become the target through which this wronged woman may strike out at all the others. She may be overreacting in her hatred for him, yet look at what she has lost—the love and companionship of Jove, the Queenship of Heaven.

In his plays Seneca displays, as in his philosophical works, a gift for aphoristic sentiments. He has at least one line worthy of standing by Homer's 'Thou too, old man, wast once happy' (spoken to the father of the dead Hector), and by Virgil's 'Even these things you will some day rejoice to remember.' Seneca's contribution to consolatory, Stoic wisdom comes at lines 656-7 of *Hercules Furens*, spoken by Amphitryon to encourage Theseus to speak of the gruesome episodes of the journey to Hell: *quae fuit durum pati, meminisse dulce est.* [What is hard to endure is pleasant to recall.]

But it is of course Hercules who gets the richest tints of Seneca's brush. Near the climax of the play, fresh from his killing of Lycus, Hercules bursts into lyric celebration:

Hither drive fat herds; whatever the fields of the Indians produce, whatever fragrant thing the Arabs gather from their trees, heap on the altars; let the rich smoke roll on high. Let wreaths of poplar bedeck our hair; but thee, O Theseus, an olive-branch, with thy own race's leaves, shall crown. The Thunderer shall my hand adore ....
(11.909-914)

And, a moment later, when Amphitryon has cautioned him to purify his hands and take some rest, Hercules continues:

Myself will I frame prayers worthy of Jupiter and me: May heaven abide in its own place, and earth and sea; may the eternal stars hold on their way unhindered; may deep peace brood upon the nations; may the harmless country's toil employ all iron, and may swords lie hid; may no raging tempest stir up the sea, no fires leap forth from angered Jove, no river, fed by winter's snows, sweep away the uptorn fields. Let poisons cease to be. Let no destructive herb swell with harmful juice. May savage and cruel tyrants rule no more. If earth is still to produce any wickedness, let her make haste, and if she is preparing any monster, let it be mine [to destroy].   (11.926-939)

Immediately after this the madness planned by Juno comes upon him. He sees his children and, thinking them the abominable spawn of Lycus, kills them. Thinking next his wife Megara is Juno, his enemy and Jove's, he kills her, then swoons and awakes in his right mind:

What horror do I see? My sons, with bloody murder destroyed, lie here, my wife lies slain. What Lycus holds sway now? Who has dared perpetrate such outrages in Thebes, though Hercules has returned? ... Whither shall I flee? Where shall I hide me, or in what land bury me? What Tanais, what Nile, what Tigris, raging with Persian torrents, what warlike Rhine or Tagus, turbid with the golden sands of Spain, can cleanse this hand? Though cold Maeotis should pour its northern sea upon me, though the whole ocean should stream along my hands, still will the deep stains cling. To what countries, man of sin, wilt thou betake thee?
(11.1159-1163, 1321-1330)

Essentially the same qualities of Hercules are displayed in Seneca's other play on this hero, the *Hercules Oetaeus.*

Seneca's career played a greater role in his writings than was usual among ancient writers. He was an exotic in Rome (he had been born in Cordoba but left Spain when he was a child); the son of a great man (his father was perhaps the foremost legist in the Roman Empire of his day), his early career was a wild mixture of successes and tribulations. While still young, Seneca was accused of plotting against the imperial family, was banished, and then recalled in triumph to become the senior of the two mentors to the young Nero. Thereafter he became the most powerful and the wealthiest man in the empire. By whim or for cause, Nero ordered him into exile once more and then commanded him to commit suicide. He died one of the most painfully drawn-out deaths on record, not unlike that of Hercules tortured into death by the robe of Nessus.

Seneca's legacy of moral essays and epistles remained as the philosophic consolation of many readers for a millennium and a half, but he did not become truly alive until the middle of the sixteenth century. Then, beginning in Italy, his plays were revived, produced, translated, imitated, and provided the basis for the modern formal drama in the Renaissances of Italy, England, Spain, and France. The tragedies of Kyd, Marlowe, Webster, and Shakespeare would be inconceivable without the model and material of Seneca. The structure of the play, the division into scenes and acts, the concept of consistent characters, and above all the tragedy expressed in deeds of violence and in rhetoric and language elevated high above daily speech—all these the Renaissance derived directly and consciously from Seneca. And, as is likely to happen even to gods or heroes, there was a second death. After Seneca's grand impact on the classical tragedy of Racine and Corneille, his influence quickly faded away. For three centuries now he has been little more than a name. Even to scholars, Latin is today normalized at the language of the mid-years, that of Virgil, Ovid, Catullus, Horace, and Lucretius. The slightly later Latin of Seneca is as strange to most scholars today as is the slightly earlier Latin of Plautus and Terence.

Seneca's overwhelming popularity at the opening of the Renaissance came from a number of accidents, all adding up to this—he was *available* for imitation, and the Greek tragic poets were not; just as, in comedy, Latin Terence and then Plautus were at hand when Aristophanes could not, generally, even be read. It is one of the great chicken vs. egg problems of history: did Seneca set the moral tone, the dramatic structure, and the melodramatic rhetoric of Elizabethan drama, and almost equally of Spanish Golden-Age tragedy and of French classical tragedy—or did these three national cultures, at abnormally expansive, bumptious stages of their history seek and soon find an appropriate avatar?

For the tastes of those eras that dislike him (including our own), Seneca is too ornately rhetorical in language and too violently melodramatic in action, as three aspects of his nature and heritage attest: he was a teacher of aesthetic beauty to a uniquely coarse emperor and empire; he followed his father and elder brother through the mazes of legistic rhetoric at a time when the lawyer's speeches were aimed at great audiences of the people rather than at select, evidence-skilled juries; his formalism is a defense against, or rather an attack upon, the chaos and irrationality of the society in which he lived. In each of these three categories he properly saw himself as the teacher, the corrector of his age, rather than, in the modern fashion, as the reflection of it.

Seneca's life and prose works reveal so strong and full a personality that one cannot help being tempted to find in his dramatic works an extension of that personality—specifically some relation between the plays and the obsessive center of his life, the character and actions of Nero, the young Master of the World. It seems not fantastic to find this relation in Seneca's choice of subjects, most of them men or women of greater than common powers, of unusual force or even cruelty verging on madness, or even, as in Hercules' case, passing over into actual violent madness. One after another the plays fall into such a pattern: the *Agamemnon*, the *Hercules Furens*, the *Medea*, the *Hippolytus*, the *Oedipus*, the *Thyestes*, the *Phoenissae*, the *Hercules Oetaeus*, the *Octavia*, the *Troades*—these stories of men or women who, endowed with more power than good sense, bring only destruction on themselves and those about them.

Hercules, in both his plays, provides clear instances. True, his madness is attributed to Juno, a source outside himself, but this is a less decisive difference from Nero's madness than it might seem. Many of Nero's outrageous acts were also in his day attributed to gods or demons, and only he himself could know to what extent he might bring these acts under his own disciplined control. The plays, then, might have served as one tool among many to provide the salutary lessons by which his enormous energies might be turned from evil outcomes to good.

And Hercules, of all Seneca's great characters, shows the closest affinities to Nero's potential for good and for evil: cruelty moving into actual violent madness, and then succeeded by acts of gentle, sweet consideration and love. Is this Seneca's portrait of Nero? Or his hope that Nero might be thus transformed? Or simply his effort to understand Nero, and to forgive whatever cruelty might yet come from him in the future?

PLATES

1
Euboian black-figure
lekythos with
Herakles and Kyknos.
Archaic Greek, mid
sixth century B.C. Clay
with glaze. H. 31.2 cm.
Collection of the Yale
University Art Gallery,
Gift of Rebecca
Darlington Stoddard
(1913. 110).*

*An asterisk denotes a detailed entry and bibliography following the plates.

2

Attic black-figure amphora with Herakles, Nessos, and Deianeira. Painter of Group E. Archaic Greek, ca. 540–530 B.C. Clay with glaze. H. 40 cm. San Antonio Museums Association (75-19 15P).*

3

Attic black-figure amphora: Side A (illustrated), Herakles and the Nemean Lion. Side B. Horseman with other figures. By the Swing Painter. Archaic Greek, ca. 530–520 B.C. Clay with glaze. H. 40.6 cm. Private collection, New York.*

4

Scarab seal with Herakles and the Kerkopes. Archaic Greek, ca. 540 B.C. Gold ring with burnt sard scarab on a swivel. L. of scarab 1.02 cm. Collection of Bowdoin College Museum of Art, Warren Collection (1928. 10).*

actual size

5
Attic black-figure
hydria with the
Apotheosis of
Herakles. Manner of
the Lysippides Painter.
Archaic Greek, ca.
530–520 B.C. Clay with
glaze. H. 46.6 cm.
Collection of the Art
Museum, Princeton
University; Trumbull–
Prime Collection
(171).*

6

Attic black-figure hydria. Body, harnessing scene. Shoulder (illustrated), Herakles, Nereus, Triton, and the Nereids. By Psiax. Archaic Greek, ca. 530 B.C. Clay with glaze. H. 47 cm. Collection of the Wadsworth Athenaeum; Ella Gallup Sumner and Mary Catlin Sumner Collection (1961. 8).

7
Relief of Herakles and the cattle of Geryon. Archaic Cypriote, ca. 520 B.C. Limestone. H. 52.0 cm. Collection of the Metropolitan Museum of Art, New York; Luigi Palma di Cesnola Collection (Myres 1368).*

8

Attic black-figure neck amphora with lid. Side A (illustrated), Herakles in the cave of Pholos. Side B, Dionysos, satyrs, and a maenad. Group of Würtzburg 199 (J. R. Guy). Archaic Greek, ca. 520–510 B.C. Clay with glaze. H. 41.6 cm. Private Collection, New York City.*

9

Attic black-figure kalpis hydria. Shoulder, Herakles attended by a satyr. In the style of the Madrid Painter. Archaic Greek, ca. 520–510 B.C. Clay with glaze. H. 34.6 cm. Collection of the Art Museum, Princeton University; Trumbull–Prime Collection (170).*

10

Attic black-figure hydria with Herakles and Triton. By the Rycroft Painter. Archaic Greek, ca. 520–510 B.C. Clay with glaze. H. 5:14 cm. Collection of Indiana University Art Museum; gift of Thomas T. Solley (77.33).

11
Attic black-figure
column krater with the
Apotheosis of
Herakles. Archaic
Greek, ca. 520–510
B.C. Clay with glaze. H.
32.3. Collection of the
Museum of Art,
Rhode Island School
of Design, museum
appropriation (29.140).

12

Attic black-figure
amphora. Side A,
Herakles Musagetes.
Side B (illustrated),
Herakles, Athena,
Ares, and Kyknos.
Painter of the Leagros
Group. Archaic Greek,
ca. 515 B.C. Clay with
glaze. H. 44. 1 cm.
Collection of the
Worcester Art Mu-
seum; Austin S.
Garver Fund (1966.63)

14

Attic black-figure oinochoe with Herakles and the Nemean Lion. Archaic Greek, ca. 520–510 B.C. Clay with glaze on a white ground. H. 13.9. Collection of the Archer M. Huntington Art Gallery, The University of Texas, Austin, James R. Dougherty, Jr. Foundation, and the Archer M. Huntington Museum Fund Purchase (1980.33).

15
Attic black-figure neck
amphora. Side A
(illustrated), Herakles,
Andromache, and
another amazon. Side
B, mounted amazons.
Archaic Greek, ca. 520
B.C, from Tarquinia.
Clay with glaze. H.
40.5 cm. Collection of
the University Mu-
seum, University of
Pennsylvania (MS 1752).

16

Attic black-figure
skyphos with Herakles
entertained by Athena.
By the Theseus Paint-
er. Archaic Greek, ca.
500 B.C. Clay with
glaze. H. 17.2 cm. Col-
lection of Mt. Holyoke
College Art Museum
(1925 BS II.3).

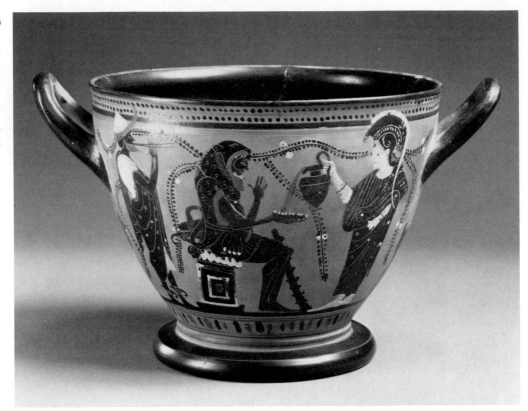

17

Attic black-figure neck amphora. Side A (illustrated), Herakles and Kyknos. Side B, Athena and Ares. By the Diosphos Painter. Archaic Greek, ca. 500 B.C. Clay with glaze. H. 20.7 cm. Collection of the Virginia Museum of Fine Arts, Williams Fund (60-11).

18

Attic black-figure skyphos with Herakles, Nereus and two Nereids. Archaic Greek, ca. 500 B.C. Clay with glaze. H. 19.4 cm. Collection of the University Museum, University of Pennsylvania (MS 5481).

19
Attic black-figure
lekythos with Herakles
and the Cretan Bull.
By the Beldam Painter.
Transitional, Greek,
500–475 B.C.
Clay with glaze. Lowie
Museum of Anthropo-
logy, University of
California at Berkeley
(835).

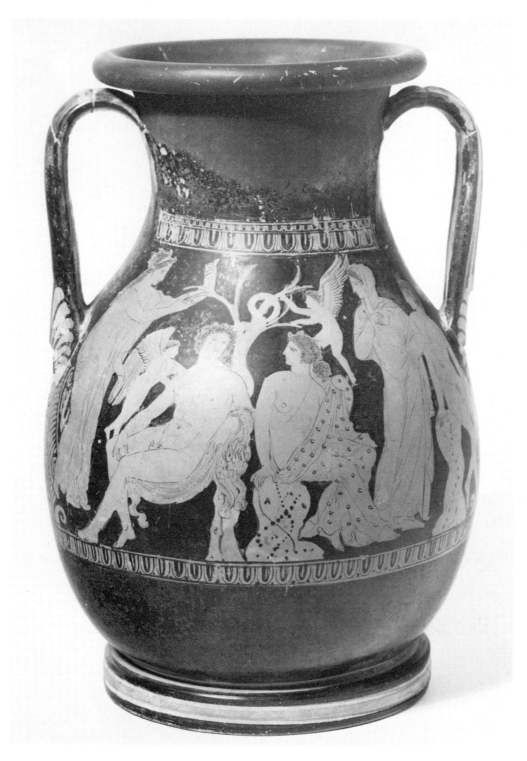

21
Attic red-figure pelike.
Side A (illustrated),
Herakles in the
Garden of the
Hesperides. Side B,
satyr, maenad and
Eros. Workshop of the
Hyppolytos Painter.
Late Classical, Greek,
ca. 375 B.C. Clay with
glaze. H. 39. 1 cm.
Collection of the Yale
University Art Gallery,
gift of Rebecca
Darlington Stoddard
(1913.138).

22

Lucanian red-figure pelike. Side A (illustrated), Herakles and the Kerkopes. Side B, Mantled youths. Close to the style of the Creusa Painter. Late Classical, Greek, ca. 380 B.C. Clay with glaze. H. 28.5 cm. Collection of the J. Paul Getty Museum; presented by Mr. and Mrs. Milton Gottlieb (81.AE.189).

23
Attic red-figure
covered pyxis with the
marriage of Herakles
and Hebe. Meleager
Painter (as attributed
by Ian McPhee) Late
Classical Greek, ca.
400–380 B.C. Clay with
glaze. H. 23 cm.
Collection of the
University Museum,
University of Penn-
sylvania (MS5462).*

24

Tetradrachm with the head of Herakles on the obverse (illustrated). Reverse, seated Zeus. Macedonian, minted in Babylonia, 326–325 B.C. by Alexander the Great. Silver. Diameter .27 cm. Collection of Torkom Demirjian.*

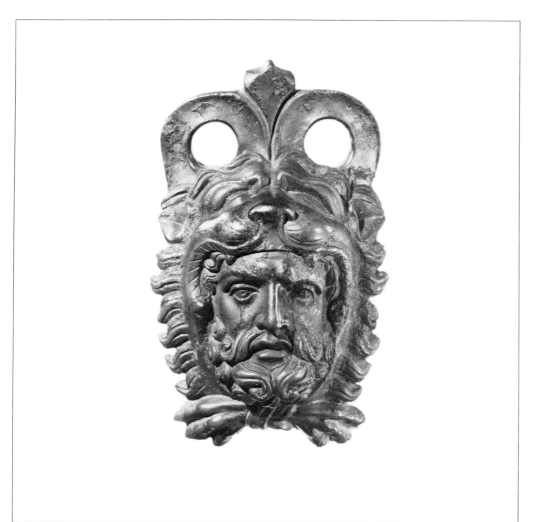

25
Situla handle attachment in the form of a Herakles head. Hellenistic Greek, late fourth century B.C. Bronze. H. 9.8 cm. Collection of the Museum of Art and Archaeology, University of Missouri (58.2).

26

Head of Herakles
with a vine wreath.
Hellenistic Greek, ca.
300 B.C. Marble. H.
18.3 cm. Collection of
the University Mu-
seum, University of
Pennsylvania, Gift of
Mrs. L. W. Drexel,
1904 (MS 4031).*

27
Head of Herakles,
wearing the Nemean
Lion skin. Etruscan,
late fourth century B.C.
Painted terracotta. H.
28.0 cm. Collection of
Robert Miller.*

28
Statuette of a
standing Herakles
brandishing his club.
Etruscan, ca. 300 B.C.
H. 16.5 cm. Collection
of the Art Museum,
Princeton University,
in honor of Francis
Follin Jones (73.3).*

29
Candelabrum finial of
a tired Herakles.
Etruscan, ca. 300 B.C.
Bronze. H. 9 cm.
Harvard University,
Alice Corrine McDaniel
Committee, the
Department of
Classics.

30

Statuette of a striding Herakles brandishing his club. Etruscan, late fourth to third century B.C. Bronze. H. 10.0 cm. Collection of Dorothy Pack.

31
Statuette of a
striding Herakles with
the Nemean Lion skin.
Etruscan, early third
century B.C. Bronze.
H. 21.5 cm. Collection
of Alan Safani.

Statuette of
Herakles standing at
rest. Etruscan, late
third to early second
century B.C. Bronze.
H. 24.0 cm. James
Coats Collection,
courtesy of Yale Uni-
versity Art Gallery
(15.3. 1973).

33
Appliqué with Eros in the guise of Herakles. Hellenistic Greek, third to second century B.C. H. 17.5 cm. James Coats Collection, courtesy of the Yale University Art Gallery (15.3.1973).

34

Jeweler's core with the Labors of Herakles. Hellenistic Greek, second century B.C. Bronze. H. 6.5 cm. Collection of the Art Museum, Princeton University, Bequest of Albert Mathias Friend, Jr. (56-101).*

35
Statuette of the
Herakles Epitrapezios,
after Lysippos.
Hellenistic Greek,
second century B.C. or
earlier. Bronze. H. 19
cm. Private Collection,
New York.

36
Oinochoe handle attachment in the form of a Herakles head. Hellenistic, Macedonian, third to second century B.C. Bronze. H. 8.5 cm. Collection of Santa Barbara Museum of Art.

37
Statuette of the infant Herakles strangling snakes. Hellenistic Greek, second century B.C., found in Egypt. Bronze. H. 12.0 cm. Collection of the Brooklyn Museum, Charles Edwin Wilbour Fund (63.185).

38
Scarab seal with
Herakles and the
broom from the
Augeian Stables.
Hellenistic. Greek.
Brown chalcedony
scarab. L. .21 cm.
Collection of Bowdoin
College Museum of
Art, Warren Collection
(1915.109).*

39
Head of Herakles
after the Weary
Herakles of Lysippos.
Late Hellenistic to
Early Roman Imperial,
about 50 B.C. to A.D.
70. Marble. H. 28 cm.
Collection of Museum
of Fine Arts, Boston,
Helen and Alice
Colburn Fund
(1976.6).*

40

Denarius of Pomponius Musa. Obverse, head of Apollo. Reverse (illustrated), Hercules Musarum. Late Republican, 68–66 B.C., minted in Rome. Silver. Dia. 2.1 cm. Collection of the American Numismatic Society (1937. 158.170).*

41
Statuette of Herakles
after the Weary
Herakles of Lysippos.
Greco-Roman, first
century B.C. to second
century A.D. Bronze.
H. 9.0 cm. Collection
of the J. Paul Getty
Museum (80-AB-77).

Statuette of Herakles
after the Weary
Herakles of Lysippos.
Greco-Roman, first
century B.C. to first
century A.D. from
Alexandria. Bronze. H.
13 cm. Private Collec-
tion, New York.

43
Statuette of the
Herakles Epitrapezios
after Lysippos. Greco-
Roman. First century
A.D. Marble. H. 43.2
cm. Collection of the
Cleveland Museum of
Art, Purchased from
the J. H. Wade Fund
(55.50).*

44

Head of the Herakles Epitrapezios used as a steelyard weight. Roman Imperial, first to second century A.D. Lead-filled bronze. H. 9.5 cm. Collection of the Cleveland Museum of Art, Norman O. Stone and Ella A. Stone Memorial Fund (71.71).

45
Mosaic fragment
with Herakles (?) and a
Phrygian. Roman Im-
perial, second to third
century A.D., from
Anagni, Italy. Poly-
chrome stone. H. 19.7.
cm. Collection of the
Lowie Museum of An-
thropology, University
of California at Ber-
keley (8.1284).*

46

Statuette of Caracalla
in the guise of
Herakles as a child.
Roman Imperial, 190–
200 A.D. after a cult
statue of 100 A.D.
Bronze. H. 28.0 cm.
Collection of the
Museum of Fine Arts,
Boston, Edwin E. Jack
Fund (1972.358).

47
Statuette of
Herakles with the
Nemean Lion skin.
Roman Imperial,
second century A.D.
Bronze. H. 10.8 cm.
Collection of Vassar
College Art Gallery
(23.8).

48

Support for a
bench or low table,
with the Nemean Lion
skin. Roman Imperial,
second century A.D.,
from the vicinity of
Rome. Italian Marble
H. 21.8 cm. The
Charles Nuffler Found-
ation, Boston.*

49
Statuette of
Herakles with the
Apples of the
Hesperides. Gallo-
Roman (?), second
century A.D. Bronze.
H. 11.5 cm. Collection
of the J. Paul Getty
Museum (71.AB.169).

50
Statuette of
Herakles and Antaios
(?). Gallo-Roman (?),
second century A.D. H.
15.5 cm. Collection of
Jerome Eisenberg.

51
Statuette of Alexander
in the guise of
Herakles. Roman Im-
perial, second century
A.D. H. 17.1 cm.
Collection of
Jerome Eisenberg.

52

Pair of earrings in the form of Herakles clubs. Roman Imperial, second to third century A.D. Gold. 3.9 cm. and 4.1 cm. Collection of the Fine Arts Museums of San Francisco, California Midwinter International Exposition (392 a-b)*

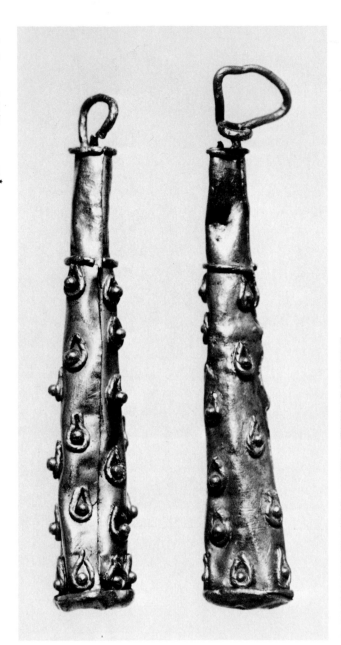

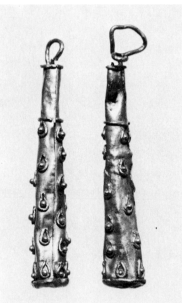

actual size

53
Head of Herakles with
a wreath. Greco-Ro-
man, late 2nd to early
3rd century A.D.
Marble. H. 15.0 cm.
Collection of Vassar
College Art Gallery
(23.73).*

54

Fragment of a sarcophagus with Omphale and a dismayed attendant. Roman Imperial, early third century A.D. Marble. H. 17.7 cm. Collection of the Museum of Art, Rhode Island School of Design, Gift of Miss Charlotte F. Dailey (02.004).*

55
Relief of Herakles carrying the Erymanthian Boar. Greco-Roman, archaistic, about 60–10 B.C. Marble. H. (as reconstructed) 69.5 cm. Collection of the Metropolitan Museum of Art, Rogers Fund, 1912 (12.157).*

56
Plaque with Herakles and the Hydra. Late antique, fourth century A.D. Bronze with copper and silver inlay. H. 18.8 cm. Collection of the Art Museum, Princeton University, the C. O. von Kienbusch, Jr. Memorial Collection (71-35).*

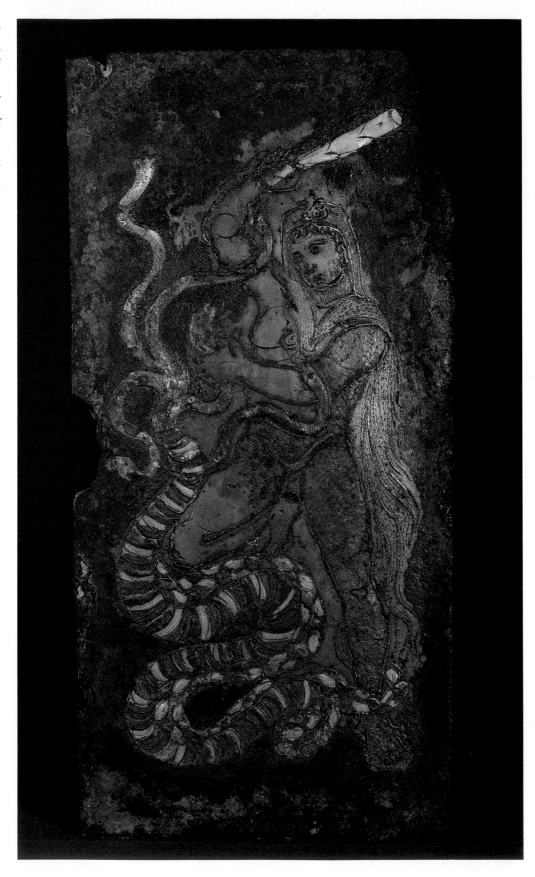

57
Relief of Herakles
Wrestling the Cretan
Bull. Late antique,
Coptic, from Egypt,
fourth century A.D.
Limestone. H. 34.0
cm. Collection of the
Brooklyn Museum,
Charles Edwin Wil-
bour Fund (61.128).*

58

Relief of Herakles with his club. Syrian, from Dura-Europos. Late antique, fourth century A.D. Limestone. Collection of Yale University Art Gallery, Yale/French Excavations at Dura-Europos 1931–1932 (1935.51).

59
Statuette of
Herakles with the
Nemean Lion. Late
antique, Syrian, ca.
fifth century A.D.
Bronze. H. 16.9 cm.
Collection of Yale
University Art Gallery,
Maitland F. Griggs
Fund (1960.57).

60

Head of a man wearing the Nemean Lion skin. Gandharan, from northwest Pakistan, fourth to fifth century A.D. Stucco with traces of red pigment. H. 21.0 cm. Collection of Indiana University Art Museum (83.20).

61
Shroud panel with the Labors of Herakles, and Dionysos. Late antique, Coptic, from Egypt, sixth century A.D. Wool and linen. H. 22.5 cm. Collection of the Metropolitan Museum of Art, Subscription Fund, 1899 (89. 18.244).

62

Sarcophagus with the
Labors of Herakles.
Roman Imperial, sec-
ond half of the second
century A.D. H. 61 cm.
L. 2.18 m. Most of the
heads restored.
Collection of
Jerome Eisenberg.

CATALOG ENTRIES

1

Euboian black-figure Lekythos with Herakles and Kyknos. Archaic Greek, mid sixth century B.C. Clay with glaze. Ca. 550 B.C. H. 31.2 cm. Collection of the Yale University Art Gallery, Gift of Rebecca Darlington Stoddard (1913. 110).

White was added for shield decoration and pattern on garments. Red was added for beards, animal manes in shoulder scene, shield and garment decoration.

Herakles enountered the brigand Kyknos, a native of Thessaly and son of Ares, at the sanctuary of Apollo at Thessalian Pagasai. It was Apollo who instructed the hero to fight the highwayman who preyed upon pilgrims bringing rich offerings to Apollo at Delphi. According to some, Ares himself at first appeared to fight alongside his son, and Herakles had to back away; then in a single combat, as on the Yale vase, Kyknos was slain.

We know more of the details of this episode than we do of Herakles' other incidental deeds, indeed more than for some of the Twelve Labors, thanks to a well-preserved early Archaic literary source. This is a brief epic poem titled *The Shield of Herakles*, which has come down to us among the works of Hesiod, but was probably written about a century later, soon after 600 B.C. An elaborate description of the hero's shield (inspired by that of Achilles' shield in *Iliad* 18) forms the centerpiece of the poem, framed by the story of Kyknos. A second poem of similar date, now lost, by the lyric poet Stesichoros (See no. 8 on Pholos in a poem of Stesichoros) told the Kyknos story in a different version.

The lekythos at Yale University was for many years assumed to be Attic and was described as such in publications as recently as a decade ago. However, Dietrich von Bothmer recognized it as belonging to a fabric distinct from, though closely dependent on, Attic black-figure, and made not far from Athens, on the island of Euboea. This is among the finest and most ambitious Euboean lekythoi, in no way inferior in potting or draughtsmanship to its Athenian contemporaries. The giveaway is rather in details of the shoulder decoration, especially the clusters of dots around the left-hand panther.

To Bothmer's stylistic observation we may add that the composition of the Kyknos scene does not fit comfortably within the narrow conventions of Attic depictions of the subject. About a third of these show the monomachy of Herakles and Kyknos with none other present. In those that include other figures, they are almost invariably the same few participants: Athena fights behind Herakles, as Ares seconds Kyknos (cf. Cat. No. 17); Zeus may appear at the center to show support for his favorite

son; and in the most elaborate versions, the combatants' wives or mothers or, exceptionally, other divinities may appear. But in no Attic example is the dueling pair flanked by unidentified 'fillers' like the four male onlookers, two nude and two draped, on our vase. The Yale lekythos brings to six the number of non-Attic fabrics that can each claim a single representation of Herakles and Kyknos: Corinthian; Chalcidian; Etruscan; Pontic (probably also made in Etruria), and Apulian black-figure. The large bird flying left that is so prominent on the Yale lekythos between the two combatants finds its nearest parallel on the Pontic amphora in Heidelberg.

Bibliography: D. von Bothmer, "Euboean Black-Figure in New York," *Metropolitan Museum Journal* 2 (1969) pp. 40–41; S. M. Burke and J. J. Pollitt (eds.), *Greek Vases at Yale* (New Haven, 1975) no. 31, with earlier bibliography (entry by J. N. Blanchard). See Bothmer's review in *Art Bulletin* 58 (1976) p. 614. On Herakles and Kyknos in Attic black-figure, see most recently H. A. Shapiro, "Herakles and Kyknos," *American Journal of Archaeology* 88 (1984) pp. 523–529. For the non-Attic black-figures, see F. Brommer, *Vasenlisten zur griechischen Heldensage*³ *(Marburg 1973)* p. 107 (the Laconian vase listed there is not Herakles and Kyknos, but a gigantomachy). The Pontic amphora: R. Hampe and E. Simon, *Griechische Sagen in der frühen etruskischen Kunst* (Mainz, 1964) plates 1–10.

A. S.

2

Attic Black-figure Amphora with Herakles, Nessos, and Deianeira. Painter of Group E. Archaic Greek, ca. 540–530 B.C. Clay with glaze. H. 40 cm. San Antonio Museums Association (75-19 15P).

White was added (mostly flaked off) for Deianeira's flesh; charioteer's chiton and animal hide. Red was added for hair and beard of Herakles and Nessos, fillet in Herakles' hair, and Deianeira's peplos.

After murdering his first wife and small children in a fit of madness, Herakles wooed and married the Aetolian princess Deianeira, daughter of King Oineus and his queen, Deipyle. Their marriage was a long and mostly happy one, even if the peripatetic hero was not often at home in Thebes. It ended only with Herakles' death, inadvertently caused by his own faithful wife. The centaur Nessos had once offered to help Deianeira across the river Evenos in Aetolia, swollen with rain. As Herakles watched from the river bank, the centaur, like others of his race unable to control his lust, tried to have his way with the young bride. The hero shot Nessos with an arrow poisoned with the blood of the Hydra, but in death Nessos took revenge. He persuaded Deianeira to save some of his blood as a love potion, should Herakles ever prove unfaithful. When, years later, the hero returned from the Peloponnese with the captive princess Iole, his distraught wife presented him with a shirt dipped in the poisonous blood. Thus did the hapless Deianeira fulfill the dark prophecy of her name ("man-destroyer").

The death of Nessos at Herakles' hand is one of the first recognizable myths to decorate an Athenian vase, the large Protoattic amphora of ca. 670 B.C. now in New York. Though unique in its imaginative rendering of the subject, this amphora introduces an important departure from the story as told by the poets: Herakles wields a sword instead of the fateful arrow. This crucial substitution raises the possibility that Herakles' killing of Nessos and his subsequent death in the poisoned shirt were not connected in the earliest versions of the story, but only by later writers, especially Sophokles in the *Trachiniai*.

The amphora in San Antonio follows the two-century tradition of Attic vases which show Herakles rescuing his wife and dispatching Nessos with the sword. Only a small handful of vases gives Herakles the bow, and of these several are non-Attic, including three Caeretan hydriae made in Etruria. The artist of the San Antonio vase has reduced the scene to its barest essentials, isolating the three principals in a blank panel devoid of any indication of setting or landscape. Herakles wears not his accustomed lion skin, but a close-fitting sleeveless chitoniskos with patterned hem, a baldric across the chest. Nessos flees the hero's sword, but wields a stone in each hand. As creatures of the wild, centaurs usually fight not with man-made weapons, but rather with whatever is ready to hand —stones, boulders, or branches. The object of this mortal combat, Deianeira, stands, as often in Archaic art, impassive, motionless, and expressionless.

The reverse panel features a generic scene especially popular on black-figure vases of the last third of the sixth century B.C., a four-horse chariot wheeling around. The fondness for horses so deeply rooted in black-figure is here combined with a new interest in movement, torsion, and three-quarter views. The small forest of legs, bristling incised manes, and attentive eyes all add to the atmosphere of excitement. The diminutive charioteer, wearing a pointed cap and animal hide over his short-sleeved chiton, is accompanied in the car by a warrior whose crested helmet above the rear horse is all we see of him.

The San Antonio amphora was assigned by Dietrich von Bothmer to Group E. This was Beazley's designation for a large and closely related group, mostly of amphoras, soon after the middle of the sixth century, B.C., which he considered might be by one hand. The *E* refers to Exekias, the great black-figure master whose art grew out of and surpassed this group.

Bibliography: J. D. Beazley, *Paralipomena Additions to Attic Black-figure Vase-painters and to Attic Red-figure Vase-painters*, 2nd ed. (Oxford, 1971); sale catalogue, Sotheby's London, 9 December 1974, no. 227; H. A. Shapiro; *Art, Myth and Culture: Greek Vases from Southern Collections* (New Orleans, 1981) 68–69. The New York Nessos amphora: K. Schefold, *Frühgriechische Sagenbilder* (Munich, 1964) pl. 23; Caeretan hydriae with Herakles and Nessos: J. M. Hemelrijk, *Caeretan Hydriae* (Mainz, 1984) pl. 70; 72–73; 82.

A. S.

3

Attic black-figure Amphora: Side A, Herakles and the Nemean Lion (illustrated). Side B. Horseman with other figures. By the Swing Painter. Archaic Greek, ca. 530–520 B.C. Clay with glaze. H. 40.6 cm. Private collection, New York.

White was added for Athena's shield device, garments of youth on side A, rider and fallen man on side B, hair and beard of old man. Red was added for hair and beard of Iolaos and Herakles, lion's mane, rim of Athena's shield and helmet fillet, hair, and garment of youth at right, side A.

Herakles' first labor was also his most popular with Greek artists, especially in the Archaic period. An invulnerable lion was sent by Hera to harass the farmers around Nemea in the northeast Peloponnese. Herakles, after discovering that all his weapons—sword, club, arrows—were useless against the beast, had in the end to strangle it with his bare hands. The invulnerable pelt, stripped from the dead lion, provided the only armor Herakles wore throughout his subsequent deeds.

Perhaps the chief interest of the scene, repeated on hundreds of Attic vases, is in the variations on the wrestling motif with which painters experimented, no doubt influenced by close observation of the favorite sport of the Athenian palestra. Herakles never fights like an animal; rather, the lion is partly humanized, often assuming improbable wrestling positions of which quadrupeds are doubtless incapable. This amphora in a New York collection, for example, displays the most popular motif of early black-figure vase painting, with hero and lion both shown upright. As always Herakles faces right, as here the lion does also, though his head, in Herakles' grasp, turns back. This schema is borrowed from slightly earlier vases of Group E. Elsewhere, the painter depicts the two opponents facing each other, like a pair of wrestlers squaring off. Contemporary with our vase are the earliest attempts at a new arrangement, with both hero and lion on the ground. In the late sixth century B.C., as on the white-ground oinochoe in Austin, Texas (Cat. No. 14), this is now the regular formula.

Holding the lion securely in a powerful armlock, Herakles thrusts his sword, only now realizing its futility. But it is clear that even without this weapon the lion has been bested, and Herakles' companions do not seem in doubt about the outcome. The youth at left is probably the hero's nephew Iolaos, holding the hero's club. Athena watches sympathetically and somewhat perfunctorily lends a hand. She is fully armed, her shield bearing a white starburst *insigne.* A second male companion behind the goddess, in short chiton and red and white mantle, cannot be named.

The reverse panel is filled with a lively, crowded composition whose exact meaning is elusive. A horseman in white, short-sleeved chitoniskos, rides to the right, as a man lies seemingly trampled beneath the horse. He is curiously clad in a sleeveless tunic with purple stripes and white shorts or loin cloth. An elderly bearded man watches impassively from the left, as three youths surround the horse, perhaps menacing the rider. Most curious of all, none of the figures is armed and no weapon appears anywhere in the scene, though the atmosphere is decidedly unfriendly. If we thus discount a military engagement or fight, this panel perhaps most likely depicts an athletic competition. In the race, a rider has lost his mount, possibly fouled by another. Friends of the loser protest the infraction, as the elderly judge looks on.

The Swing Painter was one of the most prolific artists of the finest period of black-figure art, ca. 540–520 B.C. If his draughtsmanship is not as refined as that of his contemporaries Exekias and the Amasis Painter, his subjects and their handling are seldom dull, and are often enigmatic or intriguing, as is the case with the reverse of this amphora. The Swing Painter's consistent refusal to add identifying inscriptions to his figures often adds to the difficulty of interpretation. In her definitive study of the Swing Painter, Elke Böhr places our vase, whose shape is the painter's favorite, in his middle phase, ca. 530–525 B.C.

The vase has a distinguished and long modern history, having belonged to the Fourth Baron Talbot de Malahide and his descendants at Malahide Castle, Co. Dublin, Ireland from 1849 for over a century.

Bibliography: J.D. Beazley, *Attic Black-figure Vase-Painters* (Oxford, 1956) 693, 25 *bis.;* L. Burn and R. Glynn, *Beazley Addenda* (Oxford 1983) 40; catalogue, Christie's (London), February 13–15, 1849, 302; catalogue, Christie's (London), April 4, 1976, no. 210 and pl. 19; E. Böhr, *Der Schaukelmaler* (Mainz, 1982) cat. no. 23, pl. 26. On the provenance of the vase, see J. R. Mertens, "A Black-figure Hydria of Red-figure Date," *Indiana University Art Museum Bulletin* (1979) 6, 14, n. 2. For other versions of Herakles and the Nemean Lion by the Swing Painter, see Böhr, pl. 6, 24, 34, 73c, and 142. On the transition from the standing wrestling match to the wrestling match on the ground, see J. Boardman, "Exekias," *American Journal of Archaeology* 82 (1978) 14–15.

A. S.

4

Scarab seal with Herakles and the Kerkopes. Archaic Greek, ca. 540 B.C. Gold ring with burnt sard scarab on a swivel. L. of scarab 1.02 cm. Collection of Bowdoin College Museum of Art, Warren Collection (1928. 10).

Herakles' encounter with the Kerkopes occurred during his servitude to Omphale, queen of Lydia. The Kerkopes, malicious creatures who harassed travellers, were captured by Herakles who, presumably to separate them and thus prevent further mischief, tied them each to opposite ends of a pole that he carried across his shoulders. Although they were captured, the Kerkopes' mischievous behavior so amused Herakles that in a fit of laughter he set them free.

The motif of the Kerkopes was not particularly common in Greek art, perhaps because of its nonheroic character. It was used occasionally in vase painting and in at least one other engraved gem from the Archaic period. The painter of a red-figure pelike of the early fourth century B.C. (Cat. No. 22) incorporated a picturesque touch into the scene with the Kerkopes, depicted as monkey-like creatures, shown tied to the ends of Herakles' bow.

Intaglio seals cut into gemstones were an important accessory of daily life in antiquity. Emblazoned with a symbol or emblem readily associated with the owner, they were used to seal the knotted closures of packages and documents with moist clay, thus protecting the contents from unwelcome eyes. Seals were also a means by which individuals could vouchsafe their identity or their wishes. This was a practice that reached back to remote prehistory in the Near East and Egypt and continued to

be used throughout antiquity. The appearance of the gemstone seal in classical Greece was a comparatively late manifestation of a very old tradition. The earliest Greek seals copied the form of the Egypto-Phoenician scarab, or beetle, seal and began to be produced in fair numbers around the middle of the sixth century B.C. Their popularity also took hold in Etruria where Greek craftsman from the East settled to avoid the threat of the Persian advance. This seal is typical of the scarab type produced in both Greek and Etruscan workshops in the second half of the sixth century B.C., when complex, multifigured groups, such as Herakles and the Kerkopes seen on this seal, still recalled the ambitious compositions of the Phoenician seals. Herakles motifs in general were popular among the gem carvers who used the same conceptual style for the figure seen in archaic vase painting (see especially Cat. Nos. 2 and 3). The characterization of Herakles on this seal, however, reflects a more "eastern" or Cypriote type with the lion skin forming a kilt. The hatched boarder enables it be classed with a small group of engraved gems thought to have been produced in Etruria.

Bibliography: K. Herbert, *Ancient Art in Bowdoin College* (Cambridge, MA 1964) p. 136, no. 516. J. Boardman, *Archaic Greek Gems* (London, 1968) no. 81.

J. P. U.

5

Attic black-figure hydria with the Apotheosis of Herakles. Manner of the Lysippides Painter. Archaic Greek, ca. 530–520 B.C. Clay with glaze. H. 46.6 cm. Collection of the Art Museum, Princeton University; Trumbull-Prime Collection (171).

The Hydria is mended from fragments, with some gaps filled in. White was added for women's flesh, horseman's petasos, and old man's hair and beard in shoulder scene, for horsemen's chitons in predella scene, and for shield and helmet ornaments. Purple was added for beards of Dionysos and Herakles, decoration of garments, borders of shields, and horses' manes and tails.

Herakles was the only Greek hero who underwent an apotheosis at the end of his mortal life and went to dwell among the gods on Mount Olympos. Homer already knew this story, for Odysseus, on his visit to the Underworld, remarks:

> After him [Sisyphos] I was aware of powerful Herakles; his image, that is, but he himself among the immortal gods enjoys their festivals, married to sweet-stepping Hebe. (*Odyssey* 11.601–604, trans. Richmond Lattimore)

In later times this happy fate was seen as the ultimate reward for Herakles' many labors, long suffering, and benefactions to mankind. But there is no evidence that this concept, almost Christian in its promise of a heavenly reward for good deeds on earth, was known to the Archaic Greeks. They may simply have believed that Zeus chose to elevate his favorite mortal son to divine status, marrying him to his and Hera's daughter Hebe (see Cat. No. 23). Thus was Hera reconciled with the hero whom she had plagued during his earthly career to punish his philandering father.

Greek writers do not say just how Herakles' translation to Olympos was effected. On a few early black-figure vases and a limestone pediment that adorned a small building on the Athenian Akropolis, the hero enters Olympos on foot and is presented to his father Zeus by Athena. During the second half of the sixth century, B.C., vase painters almost always preferred to have Herakles make the journey in a chariot drawn by four horses and driven by his divine patroness. In Islamic art over a millennium later, the Prophet Mohammed ascends to heaven in a chariot drawn by a fantastic female winged monster. But for the Greek hero, four noble steeds pulling a simple wooden car sufficed. (In one rare exception, the horses have wings.) Instead of arriving at Olympos, as in the scenes on foot, in the chariot scenes Herakles is shown just setting out. Thus Zeus is not present, although various other gods surround the chariot, lending a festive atmosphere to Herakles' departure on his final journey.

The hydria at Princeton presents one of the most familiar versions of the subject that decorates over two hundred black-figure vases. Both Herakles and Athena stand in the chariot as the goddess takes the reins in preparation for departure. The hero, whose body is largely hidden behind that of Athena, is most easily recognized by the club slung over his shoulder. Of the supporting cast, most obvious are Hermes, on the far side of the horses, carrying the kerykeion, and Dionysos just behind the chariot, holding a drinking horn. The ivy tendrils that spill over the left-hand third of the panel may be thought of as emanating from him. Two armed warriors also accompany the chariot: at far right may be Ares, whose ornate Boeotian shield is embossed with a rosette and device of an eagle devouring a hare. The second warrior, in the center of the panel, holding a simpler round shield decorated with white balls, is perhaps Iolaos. Finally, a young woman stands facing the departing pair, gesturing with one hand. Since no attribute marks her as one of the Olympians, she may be Hebe, a proleptic reference to the marriage the gods will celebrate just after Herakles' arrival on Olympos.

Of no less interest to the artist than these divine figures are the fine horses, standing erect and alert yet relaxed under the gentle, divine hand of Athena. That the apotheosis of Herakles by chariot instead of on foot became the predominant schema on vases may be due in no small part to the enormous fondness of black-figure painters for drawing horses. This preference is reflected on this vase in miniature on the two subsidiary friezes above and below the main panel: on the shoulder, the departure of a traveler with his horse; in the predella, four horsemen hunting a large deer.

The finest horses in Attic black-figure art were those drawn by Exekias, whose pupil the Lysippides Painter continued the tradition. This vase comes from the workshop of this younger artist and was attributed by Sir John Beazley to him. The workshop of the Lysippides Painter specialized in the production of two large pot shapes, amphoras and hydrias, though cups and other small shapes were also made. The hydrias regularly have the ambitious decorative scheme of three separate picture fields. This is in contrast to the somewhat later and more simply decorated form of hydria, the kalpis, as represented by the second Princeton vase in this exhibition (Cat. No. 9).

Bibliography: H. R. W. Smith, in *Art and Archaeology* 20 (1925) p. 119, ill.; J. D. Beazley, *Attic Black-figure Vase-Painters* (Oxford, 1956) 260. On the Introduction of Herakles: P. Mingazzini, "Le rappresentazioni vascolare del mito dell'apoteosi di Herakles," *Atti della R. Accademia Nazionale dei Lincei,* Memorie della classe di scienze morali, storiche e filologiche, Ser. 6, 1 (1925) 413-490.

A. S.

7

Relief of Herakles and the cattle of Geryon. Archaic Cypriote, ca. 520 B.C. Limestone. H. 52.0 cm. Collection of the Metropolitan Museum of Art, New York; Luigi Palma di Cesnola Collection (Myres 1368).

As J. L. (Sir John) Myres wrote in his *Handbook of the Cesnola Collection,* this narration of Herakles' tenth labor was carried out in the finest late Archaic Cypriote style, with the cattle vigorously rendered in low relief under the influence of Egyptian tomb sculpture going back to the New Kingdom and beyond, six hundred or more years before this relief was carved.

Herakles, clad only in his lion skin, advances from the left. He is brandishing his club in the raised right hand and has just shot an arrow from the bow in his outstretched left hand. The arrow has pierced the neck of Geryon's three-headed dog, Orthros, who springs forward on the relief's groundline above the cattle. In this lower register, the herdsman Eurytion, represented as a thick-set, bearded satyr or Silenos (like those on vases by the Amasis Painter) drives the cattle away from Herakles. He is protecting them with an uprooted tree and looks back to threaten the hero with a rock. The triple-bodied Geryon must have stood at the right, depicted on the same scale as Herakles, in the area at the right where the slab is broken away.

Herakles was popular on Cyprus, the more so because of his equation with the Phoenician god Melkart. The area of southern-central Cyprus radiating from Kition-Larnaca was an early outpost of Phoenician culture, and the influence of Egypt, visited by Herakles in his adventure with Busiris, was always present throughout the island. Statues of Geryon, doubtless depicted with Herakles opposite, were also popular on Cyprus, the most famous being in the Metropolitan Museum of Art, New York (see J. L. Myres, *Handbook,* pp. 204-207). Since the Geryon myth took place on the island of Erytheia in the Western Ocean, the Cypriote connection may be related to Punic cults in Spain and North Africa.

A companion piece to this statue was being exhibited by Memet the butcher in his roadside shop and "museum" at Dali (Idalion) on the limestone slopes roughly halfway between Nicosia and Larnaca, Cyprus early in the 1970s.

Bibliography: Louis P. di Cesnola, *A Descriptive Atlas of the Cesnola Collection of Cypriote Antiquities in the Metropolitan Museum of Art, New York,* Vol. 1, no. 2, (Boston, 1885) no. 912, pl. CXXII, which depicts this sculpture as sawed-off relief from the pedestal of a statue; John L. Myres, *Handbook of the Cesnola Collection of Antiquities from Cyprus* (New York, The Metropolitan Museum of Art 1914, Arno Press, 1974) pp. 234-235, no. 1368 and bibliography.

C. V.

8

Attic black-figure neck amphora with lid. Side A (illustrated), Herakles in the cave of Pholos. Side B Dionysos, Satyrs, and a Maenad. Group of Würtzburg 199 (J. R. Guy). Archaic Greek, ca. 520-510 B.C. Clay with glaze. H. 41.6 cm. Private Collection, New York City.

If Herakles' encounters with satyrs were usually friendly and tinged with good humor (see cat. no. 9), his involvement with the other principal type of Greek man/beast— the centaurs— invariably ended badly. He slew the centaur Nessos (see Cat. No. 2), who had tried to abduct his wife

Deianeira, but the centaur's revenge ultimately led to the hero's death. His meeting with Pholos and his fellow centaurs in the mountains of Arkadia began amicably enough, but soon turned sour. The centaurs had inherited a huge cask of wine with instructions to open it eventually when Herakles should arrive. Pholos himself, leader of the tribe and a creature of impeccable taste and manners, like the wise centaur Cheiron who tutored the young Achilles, welcomed Herakles with hospitality, and the two shared the newly opened wine. But the aroma inflamed Pholos' fellow centaurs, who, armed with branches and rocks, came running to the attack. (The inability of centaurs to control themselves after exposure to wine is amply illustrated by the story of the centauromachy at Peirithoos' wedding.) In the ensuing melee, Herakles slaughtered the beasts, and the hapless Pholos was accidentally killed.

The neck amphora in a New York private collection gives no apparent indication of this grim aftermath to a friendly encounter. Instead it focuses on host and guest as they prepare to share the first draft of wine. The huge pithos containing it has, following a practice known since the Bronze Age, been sunk into the earth, so that only shoulder and neck protrude. Herakles, as the guest, dips his kantharos into the jar first, while Pholos holds his at the ready. In addition to the full lion skin, belted at the waist and descending past his knees, Herakles has kept on all his weapons, a sword at his side and bow, quiver, and club slung over his shoulder— perhaps an indirect hint at the battle to come. Pholos, by contrast, is unarmed, for the branch he carries, in other contexts a centaur's favored weapon, is here hung with a dead fox and hare, spoils of the hunt. The peaceful Cheiron is often shown carrying animals in this fashion. Perhaps here they are meant as further hospitality for Herakles. A nonsense inscription seems to bubble up from the pithos, the letters like so many drops of wine. Evidently centaurs, unlike the Greeks, drank their wine neat, straight from the jar. They had not learned to tame the maddening power of wine by drinking it mixed and in moderation.

Side B does not carry the story forward, as on many vases showing the hostile or curious approach of Pholos' companions, yet it is not entirely unrelated either, for it too speaks of wine. Dionysos, patron god of wine, whose fatal gift the pithos was, stands surrounded by an entourage of two satyrs and a maenad, with vines bearing heavy bunches of grapes. The god himself holds the long curving drinking horn, or rhyton, often associated with him.

Herakles' visit to Pholos was popular in Greek art from the early Archaic period, at first more in Corinth and elsewhere than in Athens. As a principal theme for architectural sculpture it appears early in such far-flung Greek outposts as Foce del Sele, near Paestum in South Italy, and Assos in the Troad. In later sources the episode was treated as a minor *parergon* attached to Herakles' Third Labor, the capture of the Erymanthian Boar. But we know that the story was narrated in one of the most influential of early Archaic poems (now mostly lost), the *Geryoneis* of Stesichoros, who wrote in Sicily about 600 B.C. The main subject of this poem, as the title indicates, was Herakles' tenth Labor, The Cattle of Geryon (see Cat. No. 7), and the meeting with Pholos apparently took place on the return journey from the far West. Of the more than one hundred Pholos scenes on Attic vases, beginning in the last quarter of the sixth century B.C. those variants that most clearly derive from Stesichoros' poem are the drawing of wine from the pithos, as on our amphora, and a slightly later moment, Herakles and Pholos reclining together, as at a symposium. On our vase, the figures of the two principals leave no room for the ancillary figures Hermes or Athena, who appear in many black-figure Pholos scenes, nor is Pholos' cave, a regular feature on other vases, here indicated.

This amphora has been assigned by J. R. Guy to the Group of Würzburg 199, a large group of some three dozen vases, possibly all by one hand, within the Antimenean Circle. The Antimenes Painter himself introduced Herakles and Pholos to the Attic repertoire on two vases slightly earlier in date than ours (J. D. Beazley, *Attic Black-figure Vase-Painters*, Oxford, 1956, 270, 63; 273, 116).

Bibliography: Sale catalogue, Sotheby's, 16 May 1980, no. 173. On the Pholos episode in Stesichoros: P. Brize, *Die Geryoneis des Stesichoros und die frühe griechische Kunst* (Würzburg, 1980) pp. 37, 52-54, 57-58, 145-150. On Pholos in vase painting: K. Schauenburg, "Herakles bei Pholos. Zu zwei frührotfigurigen Schalen," *Mitteilungen des deutschen archaeologischen Institutes. Athenische Abteilung.* 86 (1971) pp. 43-54.

A. S.

9

Attic black-figure kalpis hydria. Shoulder, Herakles attended by a satyr. In the style of the Madrid Painter. Archaic Greek, ca. 520-510 B.C. Clay with glaze. H. 34.6 cm. Collection of the Art Museum, Princeton University; Trumbull-Prime Collection (170).

The hydria, broken and mended from fragments, has chips and a few gaps in the rim. White was added for lion's head. Purple was added for Herakles' hair and beard, satyr's beard, and decoration on Herakles' garment.

The satyr play was a special feature of fifth-century B.C. Athenian drama: a comic travesty of an epic, heroic, or tragic theme with actors dressed as satyrs playing most of the roles. A satyr play regularly followed the presentation of each tragic trilogy in the Theater of Dionysos at Athens, though the text of only one satyr play survives, Euripides' *Cyclops.* We can, however, infer from fragments of other such plays and from dozens of vase paintings inspired by satyric drama that Herakles was the genre's favorite leading man. To judge from the vases, the most popular theme revolved around the theft of Herakles' club, bow, and arrows by a band of crafty satyrs while the hero was asleep or busy holding up the earth so that Atlas could fetch for him the Apples of the Hesperides. Inevitably the larcenous satyrs are caught and punished, for many vases show Herakles leading them away bound captive or threatening them with his regained club.

More loosely dependent on satyr plays is a group of vases showing Herakles in the company of one or more satyrs, but with no apparent comic or dramatic narrative. The kalpis in Princeton illustrates one favorite motif in this group, that of the hero reclining, as if at a banquet or symposium, and being waited upon by a satyr. Herakles has hung his lion skin and quiver on the imaginary back wall and stretches out, his left elbow propped up on a striped cushion. His knotty club rests before him. A mature satyr approaches from the left, bald and with a long beard, to pour wine from an oinochoe into the kantharos in Herakles' outstretched hand. There is a note of humor in Herakles' heroic proportions which dwarf the old satyr and his correspondingly huge drinking vessel, which is far larger than the pitcher meant to fill it. Herakles' bibulousness was a *topos* of later Greek and Roman comic verse. In accordance with an Archaic convention, the hero's head is shown in profile, seeming to watch intently the pouring of the wine, while his massive torso is turned frontally, the muscles of the abdomen indicated by incision.

The shape of our vase is known as a kalpis, a term for water jar used already by Homer (*Odyssey* 7.20). It is distinguished from the more traditional hydria of black figure shape (see Cat. No. 5) by having a continuous curve from foot to rim and a single rectangular picture panel on the shoulder. Below a decorative band at handle level, here of lotus buds, the body is black. This shape was developed by potters and metalsmiths in the later sixth century B.C. and is most popular in red-figure vase-painting of the first half of the fifth century B.C. This hydria is one of the earliest examples. The small group of about a dozen vases with which the figure style can be associated, those by or near the Madrid Painter, includes several standard hydrias, but no other kalpis.

Bibliography: J. D. Beazley, *Paralipomena. Additions to Attic Black-figure Vase-painters and to Attic Red-figure Vase-painters,* 2nd ed. (Oxford, 1971); mentioned by D. von Bothmer in a review of F. Brommer, *Vasenlisten, American Journal of Archaeology* 61 (1957) 108. On Herakles in satyr plays, see F. Brommer, *Satyrspiele* Second Edition, (Berlin, 1959); ibid, "Huckepack," *J. Paul Getty Museum Journal* 6-7 (1978-1979) 139-146. On Herakles and satyrs, J. D. Beazley, "Herakles Derubato," *Apollo (Salerno)* 3-4 (1963-1964) 3-14. On the kalpis, see E. Diehl, *Die Hydria* (Mainz, 1964) 58-59.

20

A. S.

Small statue of Herakles standing. Early Transitional Period, Cypriote, ca. 490 B.C. Limestone. H. 28.1 cm. Collection of the Lowie Museum of Anthropology, University of California at Berkeley, Gift of Mrs. Phoebe Apperson Hearst (8.332).

The youthful hero is again shown wearing a tunic and the lion skin as a cap, with the forepaws tied in front of the chest and the hind legs and paws seemingly wrapped around his lower body (and tied?), although this part of the figure is now missing.

This is a somewhat rustic figure. As on the Geryon relief (Cat. No. 7), Herakles probably held the club in his raised right hand and may have grasped the bow in the extended left hand. Such a statuette could have stood alone as a votary in a temple or it could have been grouped with a similar small figure of Geryon or one of the other beings and creatures encountered by the hero.

This popular concept of Herakles in Cypriote statuary begins with the famous over-life-sized figure in the Metropolitan Museum of Art, New York (see J. L. Myres, *Handbook,* pp. 222-223, no. 1360; see also Tony Spiteris, *The Art of Cyprus,* Reynal & Co., New York, 1970, p. 158). It is older than the head in the collection of Gilbert Denman, Jr., San Antonio, Texas (see H. Hoffmann, *Ancient Art in Texas Collections,* Institute of the Arts, Rice University Houston, TX, 1970, pp. 8-11, no. 3).

Bibliography: V. Karageorghis and D. A. Amyx, *Corpus of Cypriote antiquities,* 5. In *Cypriote Antiquities in the San Francisco Bay Area Collections. Studies in Mediterranean Archaeology,* Vol. 20, no. 5) (Paul Aströms Förlag, Gothenburg, Sweden, 1974), pp. 32-33, Fig. 74; p. 65, Fig. 74.

23

C. V.

Attic red-figure covered pyxis with the marriage of Herakles and Hebe. Meleager Painter (as attributed by Ian McPhee). Late Classical Greek, ca. 380 B.C. Clay with glaze. H. 23 cm. Collection of the University Museum, University of Pennsylvania (MS5462).

The lid is mended from fragments, with chips on the rim filled in. The bowl is complete, but chipped, especially on the interior and under side. White was added for three Erotes (except wings), the incense burner, Athena's cuirass, Hebe's flesh and garments (except veil). Yellow was added for Hebe's hair and the pattern on her garment, Athena's aegis, the outlines of the Erotes, and Hebe's facial features. Relief clay (once gilded) was used for tiaras of Hera, Zeus, and Hebe, the knots on Herakles' club, the balls on the chests, Athena's spear point, and the berries on the body of the vase. In the center of the lid is a bronze band with a twisted ring.

Throughout his earthly career Herakles was plagued by the vindictive goddess Hera, because he was the offspring of Zeus' illicit affair with Herakles' mortal mother Alkmene. But after his death and passage to Mount Olympos (see Cat. No. 5), Hera's daughter Hebe was given to the hero in marriage. Not only does this wedding represent Herakles' reconciliation with Hera—the wicked stepmother turned proud mother-in-law—but it is the final step in the hero's triumph over old age and death. On earth he had wrestled Thanatos (death) for the sake of Alkestis and had fought Geras (old age) to a standstill; now a god himself, Herakles wins eternal youth by marrying the goddess who is youth personified.

The marriage of Herakles and Hebe is a very rare subject in Greek art, and the version on the pyxis in Philadelphia is perhaps the fullest and finest that has come down to us. Though it stands near the end of the Attic vase painting tradition, this vase is not closely dependent on any of its predecessors, but is an original conception of one of the last gifted red-figure artists. A black-figure vase in the Metropolitan Museum of Art, New York, shows the bridal couple in a chariot surrounded by divinities, a variant on the more popular scenes of Herakles' apotheosis (see Cat. No. 5). Only a red-figure vase in Athens about a half-century earlier than ours and still not published, might offer a prototype for the ambitious composition on the Philadelphia pyxis lid.

Herakles leads his bride, taking her wrist in a traditional Greek gesture, *cheir' epi karpo.* He has shed the lion skin in favor of a simple chlamys which leaves him essentially nude, but he retains his trusty club. Hebe is resplendent in white and gold chiton and himation, her bridal veil adjusted by a hovering Eros. To one side of the couple, a pair of women hold gifts that allude to the bride's preparations for the wedding: a loutrophoros containing water for the bridal bath and a chest with jewelry for her adornment. On the other side, a gathering of Olympian gods and their attendants prepares to witness the ceremony. Eros carries a torch, and two more torches are held by a goddess in sleeveless chiton, her hair bound in a saccos. In scenes of mortal weddings, torches indicate that the ceremony regularly took place at night. Thus our torch bearer need not be Hekate, the goddess most often so depicted, but could be Hestia, guardian of home and hearth, or perhaps Artemis, who in Athens was a special patron of marriage. Beside her sits Athena, who plays down her martial aspect for this happy occasion by pushing the Corinthian helmet back on her head and holding her spear pointed down. She is also more elaborately attired than usual, in a necklace and elaborate gold and white cuirass.

Lastly, the parents of the bride and groom, Hera and Zeus, complete the ensemble. Hera stands beside the enthroned Zeus, resting her left elbow casually on the back of his chair, as does Zeus. Each wears a diadem and holds a striped scepter, though his is the heavier and more imposing. Hera is simply dressed in a belted chiton, while her husband is nude to the waist, with a patterned cloak draped over his lap and legs. Thus he must have been depicted in the great cult image at Olympia and other monumental sculpture of the Classical period. A third Eros, painted white, accompanies the royal couple, propped against Zeus' shoulder, and in between Hera and Zeus stands a white thymiaterion, or incense burner. The artist's disarmingly mundane vision of Mount Olympos is completed by a few domestic touches interspered among the figures: rocks, birds and chests for clothing or jewelry.

The body of the pyxis, which may itself have been a wedding present, meant to hold the cosmetics of a young bride, carries no figurative decoration, but only myrtle leaves punctuated with berries which were once gilded.

The Meleager Painter, to whom the Philadelphia vase has been attributed, carried into the early fourth century B.C. the ornate or "rich style" of the late fifth century B.C. which was best exemplified by the Meidias Painter and his large circle of followers. A new element in the art of the Meleager Painter, however, is the extensive use of gilding and added yellow in combination with white, a preference that will characterize much of fourth century B.C. red-figure work. Though Herakles now is hardly the favorite subject of vase painters as he had once been, and the present scene is virtually unique, its ethos of quiet relaxation, as opposed to the action scenes of earlier times, is quite typical. This mood continues in Heraklean scenes of the following generation of Kerch vases (ca. 375–350 B.C.), which include the Yale pelike with Herakles in the Garden of the Hesperides (Cat. No. 21) and two scenes of Herakles among the gods in which Hebe herself is present.

Bibliography: *Burlington Fine Arts Club, Exhibition of Ancient Greek Art* (London, 1904) I 74, pl. 96; S. B. Luce, "A Red-Figured Pyxis," *The Museum Journal* 7 (1916) pp. 269–276; *American Journal of Archaeology* (1917) 455, Fig. 1. Black-figure hydria with Herakles and Hebe: New York, Metropolitan Museum of Art, 14.105. 10; *Attic Black-figure Vase-Painters* (Oxford, 1956) 261, 37; Kerch vases with Herakles and Hebe: K. Schefold, *Untersuchungen zu den kertscher Vasen* (Berlin, 1934) 1 on pl. 4; 3 and 4 on pl. 14.

A. S.

24

Tetradrachm with the head of Herakles on the obverse (illustrated). Reverse, seated Zeus holding eagle in right hand, scepter in left. Inscription under throne reads ΑΛΕΞΑΝΔΡΟΥ. Macedonian, minted in Babylonia 326–325 B.C. by Alexander the Great. Silver. Diameter .27 cm. Collection of Torkom Demirjian.

The first use of royal portraiture on coins for the expression of imperial power accompanies the monetary reforms of Philip II, king of Macedon. Images of Philip appearing on coins throughout the sphere of Macedonian domination gave visual testimony to Philip's conception of a united confederation of Greek city—states under Macedonian control. Philip's heir and successor, Alexander III, carried this monetary policy one step further by using a motif for his coinage which would associate his image with a divinity more closely than any ruler had ever done before. A head of Herakles wearing the lion skin headdress was chosen by Alexander to be the device for a coin minted in ten- and four-drachma denominations which was destined to be the universal coin of the Macedonian empire, supplanting all other local issues.

The choice of a Herakles device was not original; it had been used in Macedonian coinage in the late fifth century B.C. and referred to Herakles as ancestor hero of the Macedonian dynasty. Under Alexander, the Herakles motif on coins widely circulated throughout his empire stood for the might of Alexander who, like Herakles with his Labors, cleansed the world of danger and brought order out of chaos. The Herakles head which appears on the obverse of this silver tetradrachm has often been cited as an idealized representation of Alexander himself. Although this contention is not without its critics, the deep-set eyes, the slightly aquiline nose and especially the *anastole*, or upswept waves, at the forehead of our Herakles head are also features common to Alexander portraits and tend to blur the distinction between hero and ruler. But whether the actual assimilation of Herakles' persona by Alexander was intended by the die cutters of the mint or not is insignificant inasmuch as Alexander was represented as Herakles on a number of other monuments including the well-known Alexander Sarcophagus in the Archaeological Museum in Istanbul. There is no question that his association with Herakles was significantly close enough to arouse in the imagination of his subject peoples the impression that he and Herakles were one.

The figure of Zeus on the reverse recalls the posture and general format of the great cult statue of the god made for his temple at Olympia by Phidias. The reference to Zeus reiterates Philip's use of the image of the god on coins as a symbol of Macedonian rule.

Bibliography: A. Bellinger, *Essays on the Coinage of Alexander the Great* (New York, 1963).

J. P. U.

26

Head of Herakles with a vine wreath. Hellenistic Greek, ca. 300 B.C. Marble. H. 18.3 cm. Collection of the University Museum, University of Pennsylvania, Gift of Mrs. L. W. Drexel, 1904 (MS 4031).

This impressive head of the mature, full-bearded Herakles is a sculpture of great quality. Its date is difficult to establish precisely (probably in the early or late Hellenistic period). The hero seems to be standing with the lion skin draped over his lowered left arm, the club in his left hand, and perhaps a syphos or drinking-cup in his right hand. The wreath on Herakles' head suggests a position of repose after his labors. There is also the possibility, suggested in the article cited in the bibliography below, that Herakles was shown leaning slightly on his club in a pose reminiscent of the Meleager of Skopas or the earlier of the two types of the Weary Herakles identified with Lysippos.

Bibliography: Elizabeth T. Wakeley and Brunilde Sismondo Ridgway, "A Head of Herakles in the Philadelphia University Museum," *American Journal of Archaeology* 69 (1965) pp. 156–160, pl. 43 and 44.

27

C. V.

Head of Herakles, wearing the Nemean Lion skin Etruscan, late fourth century B.C. Painted terracotta. H. 28.0 cm. Collection of Robert Miller.

The art of modeling large scale sculpture in clay was an old and particularly well-developed tradition in Etruria. Varro records the name of the sculptor Vulca of Veii who was renowned for his large terracotta figures which decorated the roof of the Capitolium in Rome, perhaps toward the end of the sixth century B.C., and also mentions a clay statue of Herakles which was commonly referred to as the *Herculis Fictilis*, or "clay Herakles." Life-size portrait statues and funerary effigies were also modeled in clay, and here the Etruscan artists were able to indulge in their expressive tendencies to create deeply personal likenesses of the sitters. However, for their representations of gods and mythological characters, Etruscan artists adhered more closely to the canons of Greek art which promoted a more impersonal and aloof type of image, one seemingly more "godlike." The head of Herakles with a lion skin cap shown here reflects this detachment from the human world and illustrates the ideal of manly perfection by using the artistic vocabulary of the Classical period in Greece. The clear oval outline and simplified facial volumes of this head, and the large heavy-lidded eyes with their straight crisp brows, recall the style of the Argive sculptor Polykleitos who worked in the latter half of the fifth century B.C. Yet the dependence on Polykleitan models was not a slavish one and the sculptor of this head marked it with a definite Etruscan stamp in the overall powerful and expressive modeling of the lion skin and of the hair of Herakles, which provide an effective contrast to the almost abstract simplicity of the facial volumes. The baroque flavor of the modeling of the lion skin argues against a late fifth century B.C. date for this head and suggests that it belongs at the end of the fourth century B.C. or later. That the sculptor relied on a fifth century B.C. style long since out of date indicates archaistic tendencies.

The strict frontality of this head of Herakles and its rather formal presentation suggest that it may have originally belonged to a votive or cult statue rather than to architectural decoration.

Bibliography: Unpublished.

J. P. U.

28

Statuette of a standing Herakles brandishing his club. Etruscan, Ca. 300 B.C. H. 16.5 cm. Collection of the Art Museum, Princeton University, in honor of Francis Follin Jones (73.3).

The statuette was cast in bronze by the lost-wax method, and details were incised after casting.

This sturdy, muscular young Herakles steps to his left while brandishing his club against an unseen adversary. His upraised right hand and arm, halfway to the elbow, has been broken off; presumably, it originally held a club. His clenched, outstretched left hand once held another attribute, perhaps his bow. Herakles is beardless and nude except for his lion skin, which he wears over his head like a helmet. The lion skin's paws are knotted on his chest under his chin; its trailing lower part, bisected by a longitudinal groove, is looped like the end of a chlamys over the inside of his left elbow. Its lower end, worked into a pair of paws flanking the tail, hangs straight below the arm. Pointed edges of flanges project diagonally beyond the neck and shoulders, looking like the hinged cheekpieces of an Attic-type helmet. The lion scalp itself, squarish with rounded contours, accentuates the effect of Herakles' head being excessively large in proportion to the rest of his body. His short, compact torso rests upon

powerful legs with long thighs, prominently modeled calves and broad feet.

This statuette of the hero was probably intended to be presented in an Etruscan sanctuary, perhaps one dedicated to the hero himself, as a votive offering. It belongs to a richly varied and long-lasting series that begins in the sixth century B.C. and lasts well into the third century B.C. The type is one that follows classical Greek models fairly closely, especially those created by Lysippos and his followers and derived from their works. Comparable, among many others that could be cited, are the Herakles in Kansas City, Missouri [Nelson–Atkins Gallery, no. 49-76; S. Doeringer and D. G. Mitten, *Master Bronzes* (Fogg Art Museum, Cambridge, Mass. 1967) no. 183, p. 179], and a larger Herakles statuette in Toledo, Ohio (*Museum News, The Toledo Museum of Art* 21, 1979, 6).

Bibliography: *Record of the Art Museum, Princeton University* 33 (1974) 46 (illustrated and mentioned as a recent acquisition); *University: A Princeton Quarterly* 64 (Spring 1975) p. 6, illustrated; *Small Sculptures from the Classical World* (William Hayes Ackland Art Museum, Chapel Hill, NC, 1966) no. 55. For earlier bronze votive statuettes of Herakles, see G. Colonna, *Bronzi votivi umbro-sabellici a figura umana, I. Periodo "arcaico."* (Florence, Sausoni, 1970), nos. 193 ff., 372 ff., 404 ff. Also see J. C. Balty, "Note sur un type de l'Hercule Promachos," *Bull. des Musées royaux d'art et d'histoire, Bruxelles* 33 (1961) 2-26; *ibid;* "Dégradations successives d'un type d'Hercule italique," *Hommages à Albert Grenier I* (Brussels-Berchem, 1962) pp. 197-215. (D. J. Robert Guy supplied bibliographical references about the Princeton statuette.)

D. G. M.

34

Jeweler's core with the Labors of Herakles. Hellenistic Greek, second century B.C. Bronze. H. 6.5 cm. Collection of the Art Museum, Princeton University, Bequest of Albert Mathias Friend, Jr. (46-103).

The jeweler's core is in the form of a rectangular plaque with eight Herakles motifs in relief arranged in two horizontal rows of four motifs each. The upper row comprises a standing Herakles based on the Weary Herakles of Lysippos, a standing Herakles based on a statue type of the fourth century B.C., Herakles and the Lernaean Hydra, and Herakles and Antaios. The lower row comprises Herakles and the Nemean Lion, a standing Herakles based on the Weary Herakles of Lysippos, Herakles as an infant strangling the serpents of Hera, and Herakles swinging his club.

The repeated motif of the Weary Herakles of Lysippos suggests that the other figures on the core also may have been inspired by sculptures of Lysippos. They may be variations or reflections of statues and statue groups for a monumental sculptural cycle of Herakles' labors made by Lysippos for the Greek city of Alyzia in Akarnania in the latter part of the fourth century B.C. This group was well known, and individual motifs from it were often quoted in later Hellenistic art. The reflection of Lysippos' Alyzia cycle in the jeweler's core argues that the core was done in the second century B.C. when interest in reviving the motifs of the classical past was strong.

Jeweler's cores were used for the mass production of decorative motifs in gold or silver. Using wooden punches, a jeweler would hammer thin sheets of gold or silver over the reliefs of a minutely detailed core. The hollow reliefs were then cut out and soldered onto the surface of the object they were intended to adorn. The core at Princeton may have been part of a hoard of bronzes from Galjûb, Egypt, which contained other jeweler's cores.

Bibliography: A. Ippel, *Der Bronzefunde von Galjûb* (Berlin, 1922); E. Loeffler, "Lysippos' Labors of Herakles," *Marsyas* 6-7 (1950-1957), pp. 8-24; J. F. Kenfield, "The Princeton Core and the Alyzian Cycle" (unpublished dissertation, Princeton University, 1971); K. Weitzmann, "The Heracles Plaques of St. Peter's Cathedral, *Art Bulletin* 55 (1973), p. 6, no. 11, fig. 4; D. Amyx, *Echoes from Olympos: Reflections of Divinity in Small-scale Classical Art*, no. 27, (University Art Museum, Berkeley, 1974) and Supplement to the Catalogue, no. 27; C. Vermeule, "The Weary Herakles of Lysippos," *American Journal of Archaeology* 79 (1975) p. 331, n. 32.

J. P. U.

38

Scarab seal with Herakles and the broom from the Augeian Stables. Hellenistic Greek. Brown chalcedony scarab. L. .21 cm. Collection of Bowdoin College Museum of Art, Warren Collection (1915.109).

Herakles is represented nude with the lion skin over his back. He bends over, facing right, and holds a broom with his right hand. A cable pattern surrounds the scene. Small metal tubes project from both ends of a lengthwise drilling.

The motif of Herakles in the Augeian Stables was not often represented in Greek and Roman art. Even though it was normally included in full cycles of Herakles' Labors, it is seen as an independent motif in only a handful of gems and coins from the Hellenistic period and later. In these, the treatment of the theme differs widely, as it was freely interpreted by craftsmen. There is no evidence for some important prototype, as may have been the case for the Nemean Lion motif in vase painting (see cat. nos. 3 and 14). Depictions of Herakles using the broom to sweep the stables clean are among the most unusual, and are at variance with the story as it is related by Apollodorus (2.5., 4-5), Diodoros Siculus (4.13.3), and Pausanias (5.1.9-10). More often Herakles is shown energetically cutting a hole through the foundation of the stables for the passage of local rivers to sluice the stables clean.

The long, oval format of this engraved gem was favored in the Hellenistic Period over the wide format seen in cat. no. 4. The cramped posture of Herakles may indicate an Etruscan workshop. Despite the small size of this gem, the gem cutter was extremely skilled, as shown in the convincing representation of the nude body of Herakles. The carving is deep and allows a maximum amount of light to play over the surface, and to animate the modeling, which is dominated by strong, plastic forms.

Bibliography: K. Herbert *Ancient Art in Bowdoin College* (Cambridge, MA 1964) p. 133, no. 498.

J. P. U.

39

Head of Herakles after the Weary Herakles of Lysippos. Late Hellenistic to Early Roman Imperial, about 50 B.C. to A.D. 70. Marble. H. 28 cm. Collection of Museum of Fine Arts, Boston, Helen and Alice Colburn Fund (1976.6).

The left side of the nose was broken away, and, aside from the diagonal break at the neck and raised left shoulder, the head is in excellent condition. The surfaces have suffered some weathering or similar, natural abrasion. The marble has a yellow patina, with brown stains (from soil or metal?) on the face and the left side of the hair, neck, and beard.

Herakles' head is a free, Hellenistic rendering, of considerable quality in terms of Greek marble sculpture created after bronze prototypes, and is based on the Weary Herakles of Lysippos fashioned about 320 B.C. for the agora complex at Sikyon or the gymnasium at Argos. The statue found in the gymnasium and baths at Salamis on Cyprus, seemingly a work of the Hadrianic period, gives an excellent idea of how a more complete version of this particular figure in marble would have appeared (see *American Journal of Archaeology* 79, 1975, p. 325, no. 4, pl. 51, fig. 2). This head and the Greco-Roman statue from Salamis, in the Cyprus Museum at Nicosia, may approximate the scale of the Lysippic original, although that versatile and prolific master may have also cast a version considerably (double-sized?) larger than these slightly under life-sized figures.

Heads in the class closest to the statue by Lysippos are free from the strain and pathos found in Pergamene revisions of the subject, which show the hero leaning on his club, with the Apples of the Hesperides held behind him in his right hand.

Bibliography: C. Vermeule, "The Weary Herakles of Lysippos," *American Journal of Archaeology* 79 (1975) p. 325, no. 7. M. B. Comstock and C. C. Vermeule, *Sculpture in Stone, The Greek, Roman and Etruscan Collections of the Museum of Fine Arts, Boston* (Museum of Fine Arts, Boston, 1976) p. 66, no. 104A; Erika B. Harnett. In *Aspects of Ancient Greece* (Allentown Art Museum, Allentown, PA, 1979) pp. 166-167, no. 81, dated "second century A.D.".

C. V.

40

Denarius of Pomponius Musa. Obverse, head of Apollo. Reverse (illustrated), Hercules Musarum. Late Republican, 68-66 B.C., minted in Rome. Silver. Dia. 2.1 cm. Collection of the American Numismatic Society (1937. 158.170).

Pomponius Musa was one of three mint officials, known collectively as the *tresviri monetalis,* who were appointed by the senate to issue money and supervise the national mint. Musa was active in this office during the decade of the sixties B.C. of the late Republican period. At that time it was customary for the senatorial moneyers to promote themselves through coin devices which were personally meaningful, even though it was also understood that these coins were minted under general senatorial control. Musa issued a rather long series of silver denarii of outstanding artistic quality emblazoned with a head of Apollo on the obverse and images of each of the Muses on the reverse, an obvious visual pun on Musa's name, accompanied by the legend "Musarum," an equally obvious verbal pun meaning "Musa's" as well as "of the Muse's." An unusual denarius thought to belong to this series is one showing Herakles on the reverse playing the lyre with the legend, "Hercules Musarum."

Herakles' association with the Muses is vague although it can be documented in at least one statue group of Apollo, Herakles, and the Muses from Messene in Greece.

Representations of Herakles playing the lyre, as Musagetes, or of the Muses, are more frequently encountered, but only in Greek vase painting (Cat. No. 12) and occasionally on gems; the motif is unknown in monumental Greek art. The symbol chosen by Q. Pomponius Musa to decorate the reverse of his denarius was unquestionably unusual. Yet there was a temple in Rome dedicated to Hercules Musarum. The temple was set up by M. Fulvius Nobilior in 186 B.C, on the occasion of a military triumph, and housed a group of nine statues of the Muses which Fulvius had looted from the Greek city of Ambrakia. That they were part of war booty made them appropriate dedications to Herakles since a percentage of the spoils of a campaign was customarily offered to him. He then served as their protector, earning the name Herakles of the Muses. More than a hundred years later the temple of Hercules Musarum and its Muses served as a convenient symbol for Pomponius Musa who could not only stress the privileged association of his name with that of Apollo, god of the Muses, but also with Herakles who, in the late Republican period, was the fashionable ancestor of many republican families.

The source of the motif of the music-making Herakles on Musa's denarius can only be conjectured. While it is not impossible that Musa fabricated the image himself, we must also ask whether there was a statue of Herakles Musagetes accompanying the Muses in the temple of Hercules Musarum.

Bibliography: L. Richardson, *American Journal of Archaeology* 81 (1977) p. 355 ff.; for the entire series of denarii, see E. A. Sydenham, *The Coinage of the Roman Republic* (London, 1952) nos. 810–823.

J. P. U.

43

Statuette of the Herakles Epitrapezios after Lysippos. Greco-Roman. First century A.D. Marble. H. 43.2 cm. Collection of the Cleveland Museum of Art, Purchased from the J. H. Wade Fund (55.50).

As Franklin Plotinus Johnson wrote nearly 60 years ago, the bronze (or silver) Herakles *Epitrapezios* ("on the table") is the only work of Lysippos that can be identified with certainty on external evidence. Martial wrote in the reign of Domitian (81 to 96 A.D.) about a small bronze statuette in the possession of Novius Vindex, "I read (the name) Lysippos; I thought it was (the work) of Pheidias." The description and this marble version show that the hero was seated on a rock over which the lion skin was placed. In addition, we know he held the club in his left hand and a cup in the raised, extended right hand.

The Cleveland copy has faithfully caught the details of the aging hero's head as he looks upward, and the strong musculature of his body. Small statues such as this were popular in the rockwork gardens of Roman villas like those around the Bay of Naples.

Bibliography: *Handbook of the Cleveland Museum of Art* (Cleveland Museum of Art, Cleveland, OH, 1958) Fig. 33, F. P. Johnson, *Lysippos* (Duke University Press, Durham, NC, 1927) pp. 98–104.

C. V.

45

Mosaic fragment with Herakles (?) and a Phrygian. Roman Imperial, second to third century A.D., from Anagni, Italy. Polychrome stone. H. 19.7. Collection of the Lowie Museum of Anthropology, University of California at Berkeley (8.1284).

This fragment preserves the head and part of the upper bodies of two figures. The first, beardless and viewed in profile facing right, wears a Phrygian cap and carries a shield and spear. The second beardless figure advances toward the right, but turns and faces left as he lifts his left hand; he wears a girdled tunic and an animal skin helmet with the paws tied below his neck. He holds a bow and carries arrows in a quiver slung behind his back.

The subject of this mosaic fragment is unclear. It has been interpreted as a representation of Roman legionaires, one of whom is a *signifier*, or standard-bearer, wearing the characteristic bear skin cap. More likely, however, the subject is mythological, given the presence of a figure who can only be a barbarian, specified in classical art by Phrygian dress. The presence of a Phrygian cannot be explained within the context of the Roman army, nor would one expect to find a *signifier* depicted as an archer. Although the animal skin helmet is too generalized to be recognized as belonging to a lion, it would be reasonable to see Herakles in the figure who hastens forward with an eager glance backward, as he reaches for an arrow. The presence of the Phrygian, suggesting a locale in Asia Minor, could be taken to indicate a depiction of Herakles' attack on Troy. An alternative explanation has been suggested by Cornelius Vermeule: this mosaic fragment may have belonged to a scene symbolizing a city in Phrygia such as Heraklea Pontica.

Bibliography: M. Del Chiaro, *Roman Art in West Coast Collections* (Santa Barbara, CA, 1973) no. 47; F. Stern, *The Labors of Herakles on Antiquities in West Coast Collections* (Eugene, OR, 1976) no. 16.

J. P. U.

48

Support for a bench, or low table, with the Nemean Lion Skin. Roman Imperial, second century A.D., from the vicinity of Rome. Italian Marble H. 21.8 cm. The Charles Nuffler Foundation, Boston.

The marble has been broken across the middle of the pillar or rectangular support, and there is chipping around the lion's head and the knotted skin, including the paw at the viewer's left. The back is cut roughly flat, sculpted at the top and with a rectangular wedge at the upper rear, as if designed for holding a table or as a bench-support.

This support can be completed from a pair of similar sculptures, terminating in large feline paws on their plinths. These two marbles are currently beneath a Nereid sarcophagus in the Belvedere of the Vatican Museums. (See W. Amelung, *Die Sculpturen des Vaticanischen Museums,* Vol. 2, George Reimer, Berlin, 1908 p. 253, nos. 91a and b, pl. 23).

Bibliography: Margaret Ellen Mayo, *Ancient Art* (The Summa Galleries, Inc., Catalogue 3, Beverly Hills, CA, 1977) back cover in color and p. 2 no. 2; C. Vermeule, "Bench and Table Supports:

Roman Egypt and Beyond," *Studies in Ancient Egypt, the Aegean, and the Sudan* (Department of Egyptian and Ancient Near Eastern Art, Museum of Fine Arts, Boston, 1981) pp. 180, 189, Figs. 1 and 2, the Vatican supports.

C. V.

52

Pair of earrings in the form of Herakles clubs. Roman Imperial, second to third century A.D. Gold. 3.9 cm. and 4.1 cm. Collection of the Fine Arts Museums of San Francisco, California Midwinter International Exposition (392 a-b)

The earrings are canonical tubes closed at the narrow end by ferrules set off at the bottom by a horizontal wire rib; separately wrought wire loops are attached to the ferrule; repousse work and small granules suggest the knots of the club; the end is closed by a worked disk.

The use of Herakles motifs in jewelry was fairly widespread in classical antiquity. The "Herakles knot" was a familiar feature in many types of Greek necklaces, diadems, and bracelets, and Herakles' club provided necklaces with decorative finials for their closures from the fourth century B.C. onward. The motif of the Herakles club for earrings, however, is documented only in Roman jewelry. Although difficult to date on stylistic grounds, the majority of the extant Herakles' club earrings come from tombs whose contexts cluster around the second to third century A.D. Such earrings have been found throughout the Roman empire from Britain to the Black Sea, and show varying degrees of ornamentation. The earrings shown here represent one of the more simple types known. In other examples, such as the earrings from Birdoswald now in the Carlisle Museum, England, the knots of the club are surrounded by fine granulation and the woody texture is similarly highlighted. In the most elaborate examples, glass paste imitating tiny gems, such as cornelian, replaces the knots which on our earrings are described only by single minute granules of gold.

The use of a Herakles club as an independent motif in jewelry, rather than as part of a necklace, may associate the wearer in some way with Omphale, the Lydian queen who held Herakles in servitude and compelled him to exchange clothes with her. A Roman portrait statue of a woman dressed as Omphale, nude but for Herakles' lion skin and club, dates to the same period as our earrings and may refer to a domestic cult of Hercules; perhaps the earrings served in a more decorative way to associate the wearer with his protection. This does seem likely to have been the case where a Herakles club was worn on a chain as an amulet, doubtless the fate of many earrings after one from the pair was lost.

Bibliography: F. Stern, *The Labors of Herakles in West Coast Collections* (Eugene, OR, 1976) no. 44; see also D. Charlesworth, *Antiquaries Journal* 57 (1977) 323 for the most recent discussion with predeeding bibliography.

J. P. U.

53

Head of Herakles with a wreath. Greco-Roman, late 2nd to early 3rd century A.D. Marble. H. 15.0 cm. Collection of Vassar College Art Gallery 23.73).

This Greco-Roman head is unusual for the deep drilling of the beard and the hollowed eyes, which could have been inset in another material. The wreath in the hair recalls other representations of Herakles, and this head probably reflects a Hellenistic image of the hero in bronze with inlaid eyes.

There is, however (and the damages make determination difficult), the possibility that another divine being is represented here, perhaps Silvanus, god of woodlands and their produce.

Bibliography: Fogg Museum of Art, 1932. 56. 125: G. M. A. Haufmann, D. G. Mitten, C. C. Vermeule, *et al., Stone Sculptures. the Greek, Roman, and Etruscan Collections of Harvard Univeristy* (Harvard University Art Museums, Cambridge, MA, 1986) no. V 1; F. Poulsen, *Catalogue of Ancient Sculpture in the Ny Carlsberg Glyptotek* (Ny Carlsberg Glyptotek, Copenhagen, 1951) pp. 251-252, nos. 492, 493, pl. XXXVII.

C. V.

54

Fragment of a sarcophagus with Omphale and a dismayed attendant. Roman Imperial, early third century A.D. Marble. H. 17.7 cm. Collection of the Museum of Art, Rhode Island School of Design, Gift of Miss Charlotte F. Dailey (02.004).

Omphale, Queen of Lydia (who purchased Herakles as her slave after he had committed murder and offenses against Zeus and Apollo) dressed in the skin of the Nemean Lion. Some say she put Herakles into dresses and female nightgowns. On this relief from a rectangular Roman sarcophagus, she looks out at us with the lion's scalp on her head, while an attendant appears disturbed by these goings-on. Maybe the second woman had to surrender part of her wardrobe for use by Herakles. It is difficult, from the paucity of parallels, to know what other scenes were on this side of the sarcophagus, but surely they were involved with larger aspects of the story of Herakles.

The symbolism of the powerful strongman enslaved by a woman of renown must have something to do with Stoic or Neo-Platonic notions current in the early third century A.D., about the quirks of fate and death, visual themes appropriate to a marble coffin. While the emperors of this period, notably Septimius Severus (193-211 A.D.) and his son Caracalla (198-217 A.D.) adored Herakles and Dionysos, the later Severan boy-emperors, Elagabalus (218-222 A.D.) and Severus Alexander (222-235 A.D.), who were dominated by the female members of their family, were not averse to seeing these royal ladies sculpted as Omphale, dressed in nothing but the Nemean Lion's skin: see Guido Kaschnitz-Weinberg, *Sculpture del Magazzino del Museo Vaticano*, Vol. 1 (Pontificia Accademia Romana di Archeologia, Vatican City, 1937) pp. 295-296, no. 727, Vol. 2 or II pl. CXIII.

Bibliography: B. S. Ridgway, *Catalogue of the Classical Collection of Sculpture* (Museum of Art, Rhode Island School of Design, Providence, RI, 1972) p. 103, p. 219, no. 40.

C. V.

55

Relief of Herakles carrying the Erymanthian Boar. Greco-Roman, archaistic, about 60-10 B.C. Marble. H. (as reconstructed) 69.5 cm. Collection of the Metropolitan Museum of Art, Rogers Fund, 1912 (12.157).

Although much of the background of this relief has been restored (only the lower right corner being ancient), this representation of the hero's Third Labor gives the appearance of having been copied from the metope of a late Archaic temple of Sicily. Since the school of sculptors, headed by Pasiteles, who worked in Rome in various academic versions of older Greek styles, came from this part of the world, it seems likely they brought models for a pseudo-Archaic or Archaistic set of the Labors of Herakles with them.

Whether this relief came from Taranto or the heart of Rome, as variously reported (G. M. A. Richter, *Catalogue of Greek Sculptures* p. 20; see bibliography, below), we can imagine this creation after a work of around 500 to 490 B.C. as having been one of a series of plaques (the Labors?) on a public or private building of the time of Caesar, Cicero, and the family of Augustus.

Although Herakles captured the Erymanthian Boar in the snows of the North and brought him alive to frighten King Eurystheus at Mycenae, the animal seems thoroughly tranquilized here.

Bibliography: G. M. A. Richter (*Metropolitan Museum of Art, New York, Catalogue of Greek Sculptures,*); *Catalogue of Greek Sculptures* (Harvard University Press, Cambridge, MA, 1954) pp. 19-20, no. 24, pl. XXIII, d.

C. V.

56

Plaque with Herakles and the Hydra. Late antique, fourth century A.D. Bronze with copper and silver inlay. H. 18.8 cm. Collection of the Art Museum, Princeton University, the C. O. von Kienbusch, Jr. Memorial Collection (71-35).

A section from the left edge of the plaque and its upper right corner are missing. The figure of Herakles battling the Hydra is rendered in a mixture of sheet metal inlays and overlays of differing hues, and incised contours, also partly filled with metal. Herakles' body, as well as some of the alternating scales of the Hydra, are rendered in reddish copper. The lion skin is shown in a more yellowish metal; it is textured throughout by incised stippling and longitudinal contours to represent the pelt. Others of the Hydra's scales are inlaid in what appear to be contrasting alloys of silver or even niello, the shiny black alloy of silver and sulfur that was often used to form a background for lighter metal inlays on silver vessels in late antiquity; the presence of niello in this piece, however, has yet to be completely substantiated. Silver forms the club and the five snaky heads of the Hydra. While a few of the inlaid elements have been worn through or are missing, the overall vivid coloristic composition and effect of the picture remains intact.

The artist has depicted Herakles in a frontal pose, his right knee braced into the topmost fold of the Hydra's coiling body, his weight placed upon his vertical left leg, frontally foreshortened. He wears the skin of the Nemean Lion as both head covering, knotted on his breast, and as a cloak, which trails down his left side as far as his ankle. With his left arm, he reaches across his torso to grasp the neck of one of the Hydra's five heads, while the heads adjacent on either side writhe upward to attack him. The striped tail of the Hydra has even wrapped itself, constrictorlike, around Herakles' left ankle. Herakles brandishes his club with his left hand, bending it back over his head in preparation for a downward blow. The Hydra's fourth head rises vertically from the left corner of the plaque, while the fifth curls downward and outward.

The entire composition is highly dynamic, with complex overlapping and intertwining forms. Still highly polychrome in effect, the original appearance must have been even more dramatic. The technique of "painting in metal" through differing alloys and colors of metallic inlays is an ancient one, appearing already in early Eighteenth Dynasty royal weapons (axe and dagger of Queen Ahhotep, Cairo Museum) and in the magnificent inlaid bronze daggers and silver vessels from the Shaft Graves at Mycenae and elsewhere in Bronze Age Greece (ca. 1600-1200 B.C.). A similar, more developed technique, of which the Princeton plaque is a fine example, flourished especially in the late Roman and early Byzantine cultural centers of the eastern Mediterranean, in inlaid scenes with black niello backgrounds on elaborate silver dishes such as some of those from the Kaiseraugst Treasure of the early fourth century A.D., found at Augst on the south bank of the Rhine just east of Basel. The technique is also similar in its effect to that of elaborate scenes in *opus sectile* composed of cutout elements in multicolored marbles, such as those in the basilica of Junius Bassus in Ostia.

The plaque was probably one of a set of twelve that depicted the cycle of the hero's canonical labors, such as the cycle of ivory plaques on St. Peter's Cathedra discussed by Weitzmann (see bibliography). No satisfactory explanation for what this larger object would have been, however, has yet been suggested. Nevertheless, the Princeton plaque remains one of the most impressive virtuoso examples of this technique to have come down to us, as well as a superb representative of the continuing vitality of the three-dimensional classical tradition of pictorial narrative in late antiquity.

Bibliography: H. Beck and P. C. Bol (eds.), *Spätantike und frühes Christentum* (Liebighaus, Museum alter Plastik, Frankfurt am Main, 1983) p. 585, no. 181, illus.; W. Eugene Kleinbauer, "A Byzantine revival: The inlaid bronze doors of Constantinople," *Archaeology* 29 (1976) pp. 22-23, 27-29, 26 (reproduced in color); *The Metropolitan Museum of Art Bulletin* 25 (2) (1977) p. 29 (enlarged color reproduction); *Record of the Art Museum, Princeton University* 31 (1) (1972) p. 30 (noted as recent acquisition and illustrated); Kathleen J. Shelton. In *Age of Spirituality: Late Antique and Early Christian Art, Third to Seventh Century* (New York, Metropolitan Museum of Art, 1979) cat. no. 137, pp. 160-161; illustrated, also in color, pl. III; K. Weitzman "The Heracles Plaques of St. Peter's Cathedral"; "*Art Bulletin,* 55 (1973) pp. 24-26, Fig. 48. For sources and examples of the Labors of Herakles, cf. Weitzmann, *op. cit., passim.*

D. G. M.

57

Relief of Herakles Wrestling the Cretan Bull. Late antique, Coptic, from Egypt, fourth century A.D. Limestone. H. 34.0 cm. Collection of the Brooklyn Museum, Charles Edwin Wilbour Fund (61.128).

The sculptors of buildings, including tombs, in Late Antique Egypt included vignettes from older Greco-Roman myths because they could suggest many things to different people, from the foibles of the pagan past to the heroes of the ancient Near East and the Old Testament. Since Herakles captured the bull on Crete and let it loose in Attica, the labor of a hero who roamed all over the ancient world from Gibraltar to Asia Minor, from Russia to Egypt, made a perfect decorative motif amid the curling acanthus-stems and leaves of an architectural frieze.

Here the style is a flattening and stiffening of undercut carving popular in the peopled scrollwork of friezes on big Roman buildings of the third and fourth centuries A.D. Between 180 and 220 A.D. such carving was used widely in the Gymnasium and other public buildings at Salamis on Cyprus.

Bibliography: V. Karageorghis, C. C. Vermeule, *Salamis Vol. 2, Sculptures from Salamis,* Part II (Department of Antiquities, Republic of Cyprus, Nicosia, 1966) pp. 5-10, 25, no. 91, pl. XI, 2.

C. V.